Alfred Henry Lloyd

Philosophy of History

An Introduction to the Philosophical Study of Politics

Alfred Henry Lloyd

Philosophy of History
An Introduction to the Philosophical Study of Politics

ISBN/EAN: 9783337073497

Printed in Europe, USA, Canada, Australia, Japan

Cover: Foto ©Thomas Meinert / pixelio.de

More available books at **www.hansebooks.com**

PHILOSOPHY OF HISTORY

AN INTRODUCTION

TO THE

PHILOSOPHICAL STUDY OF POLITICS

BY

ALFRED H. LLOYD

AUTHOR OF "CITIZENSHIP AND SALVATION" AND
"DYNAMIC IDEALISM"

ANN ARBOR
GEORGE WAHR, PUBLISHER
1899

PREFACE.

A FINISHED book must always be to its author only a program for future work. Particularly is this true of a book that owes its being to the discussions of a university lecture-room. Thus, the present volume, growing out of work with students in political philosophy and the philosophy of history is only a preparation for something more extensive and philosophically more satisfying, and publishing it as I do for the use of my own students, who must always be more devoted to thinking than to knowing, I would have it viewed in no other light.

And this is my second attempt to formulate a view of history, the first being in *Citizenship and Salvation*.* If the present formulation does not help the understanding of the earlier one I shall be greatly disappointed. The view itself is not a new one, but an in-

* Citizenship and Salvation, or Greek and Jew. A Study in the Philosophy of History. Little Brown & Co. 1897.

dividual's statement always has some chance of being serviceable.

A. H. L.

ANN ARBOR, MICHIGAN,
August, 1899.

CONTENTS.

	PAGE
INTRODUCTION	9

Part I.
DATA OF HISTORY.

CHAPTER		
I.	TIME	21
II.	CAUSATION	37
III.	NATURE	54
IV.	INDIVIDUALITY	59
V.	PROGRESS	80

Part II.
SOCIETY AND SOCIAL CHANGE.

VI.	THE GROUP IN GENERAL	97
VII.	THE HUMAN GROUP OR SOCIETY	102
VIII.	THE DOUBLE RESPONSIBILITY OF SOCIETY . .	120
IX.	THE STAGES OF SOCIETY'S ACTIVITY . . .	131
X.	THE PROCESS OF SOCIETY'S ALIENATION FROM ITSELF	143
XI.	THE PROCESS OF SOCIETY'S RESTORATION TO ITSELF	168
XII.	PROGRESS IN THE ACTIVITY OF SOCIETY . .	201

Part III.

HISTORICAL STUDIES.

XIII.	REASON AND RELIGION	211
XIV.	GOOD AND EVIL	222
XV.	REVOLUTION	234
XVI.	THE GREAT MAN	240
CONCLUSION		249
INDEX		253

PHILOSOPHY OF HISTORY

INTRODUCTION.

PHILOSOPHY is always to be distinguished from science. Science, judged according to her own account of herself, is the interest in knowledge just for knowledge's sake, but philosophy is interested in knowledge not as mere knowledge but as motive. According to philosophy knowledge must be more than formally true and consistent; it must be also liberative. Knowledge for knowledge's sake is necessarily abstract; or, if seeming concrete, it is so with reference to something to which the knower is denied any vital relation, and to be concrete on these terms is to reach the very summits of abstraction. Only knowledge as the truth that sets you free, that moves not the knowing but the living and acting self to expression, is strictly concrete. The philosopher, just in view of his interest in a knowledge that is liberative and concrete is to be classed with the seekers after the wisdom of life, with the laborers and the reformers in society, with those whose little knowledge is ever a great striving and whose striving never fails to awaken the wish for greater knowledge. His seeking for knowledge is their seeking become special and intense and responsible not to any limited sphere of activity but to the universe. If he turns to science—and he always does and always must—it is solely that he may apply and animate scientific ideas.

Of course scientific ideas can not be applied and animated until all the separate sciences are made fully responsible to each other, until they have been tested, each one and all of them, as theories of the universe, or finally until they have been brought under a single organizing and transfiguring idea, but in spite of this duty to interpret and organize the sciences the philosopher never loses his interest in a truth that liberates. The history of philosophy is but a record of the ideas, both in their temporal sequence and in their logical relations, that have been the central and controlling motives of man's progress.

But the philosophy of history, which is the concern of this book, is not exactly the criticism and interpretation of a particular science in the light of a theory of the universe, as what has been said so far might seem to imply. It is not this, however, for the simple reason that history is to be regarded rather as a method in all the sciences than as a science by itself. True, when we speak of history, we usually understand that the account of man's progress and civilization is intended, but it is true also that the history of man, although a special branch of investigation, is after all only a means or a method in the science of politics. To man the story of his own achievements is so absorbing that he allows himself for a time to be diverted from the end that the story really has in view, but this diversion neither prevents the ultimate subordination of the history of civilization to the science of politics, nor makes the relation of the two in any essential way different from that of any history to any science. Accordingly, although the direct interest here is to be in the peculiar history of man and particularly in the history of civilized man, and although the chief illustrations of such principles as may be brought forward are to be taken from man's history, any reader, who fails to find, at least between the lines, a philosophy of history in a more general sense, will have failed to get all that this book is meant to contribute.

To examine history philosophically, as the foregoing account of philosophy implies, is to examine the fundamental data of history, the general facts or the general principles that every historian takes for granted or is very likely to take for granted, and in the examination to determine how far they are really and consistently thinkable. The philosopher of history, like the philosopher in general, must see history as something in which he and his fellows have had, have, and are to have an active share. He must be able to say of history: "That am I" or "That are we," and because his responsibility is very broad and very deep he can not do this without the most thoroughgoing criticism. The mere story may interest or entertain him, but it can not move him, until it is found to be perfectly rational, or until, as the same thing, it reflects his life and draws him into itself. Not only must he be able to rationalize his history as a series of events but also he must know what history as such is, what its meaning to experience and what its place in the universe. The historian, for example, is ordinarily content to leave unexamined the facts of time, causation, individuality, progress, but the philosopher, eager fully to understand history, can find no things so important and so absorbing.

Some have insisted that the philosophy of history has to busy itself with universal history and this is without doubt true, but there is the intensive as well as the extensive way of studying universal history. Determine what time is, what an event in time is, what causation and individuality and progress are, and what society is, and universal history is bound to stand before you. Of course to reach these determinations you need all the evidence or illustration from actual historical records that you can command, but the philosophy of history itself is free from any necessity of a complete record of history. The case is possibly somewhat like that, familiar to the biologist, of the organism that recapitulates its own evolution but not fully and not literally. As organic life is greater than any special stages of its own growth, so history as an affair of events and of individuals in general is greater than any existing record.

The objection is often raised that to assume,

as philosophy does, that history can be reduced to a formula, that is to say, that history is the manifestation of a law, not the mere achievement of man living in the past and struggling against all sorts of obstacles, is to rob human activity of spontaneity and responsibility, but this objection is certainly very shallow or very near-sighted, for exactly the opposite must be r ue. Thus, spontaneity and responsibility are certainly affairs wholly of the present, not of the past, and just for the sake of the present, that the present may be free, having something to guide its activity and to establish its experience, it is necessary that the past should appear in no other light than that of a law. Had not those who have gone lived in a law, and were we now unable to know the law in which they lived, our freedom would be about as empty and as useless as could possibly be imagined. Moreover, if it is true, as we all believe, nay, as we all know, that through the course of organic life, or more narrowly of human progress, the all-pervading and all-controlling idea has been to rationalize experience, most assuredly there is no cause even for the past to complain and much less for any of us to complain in its behalf, when the life that was is found to have been rational or according to some law. The present, finding the past a lawful past, does but say to those that were: "You have builded even better than you knew; the longing for law, for unity, in your life was no idle longing, since what you sought I find to have been fulfilled." Where motive and result are one, freedom need not be questioned.

And also this is to be said here, although in later pages the matter will have to be treated at greater length. The life of the past and the life of the present are wrongly thought of as two lives, as different or unrelated. Not those that are now gone once lived and we live, but they and we are living; they in us and we with them. When, looking over the past, we think of freedom or spontaneity or responsibility as belonging to the makers of the past, we are in a very real and a very important sense, in a sense that is not a poetic fancy but a wholly prosaic experience, turning the creatures of yesterday into our own contemporaries. More than one writer has been keen enough to see that contemporaneity sets the temporal bounds of history, and a more important principle for the philosophy of history would be hard to find.

It is Hegel, I think, who has defined the philosophy of history as comprehension of the logic of human events, and with this definition no fault can be found, if the final making of history be recognized as the true philosopher's motive. An abstract logic is one thing; a philosophy of history, quite another. But, not to dwell upon this, there is a way to study history philosophically that ought to be mentioned here, although it is not to be the way of this book. Thus, one may study the philosophical ideas, that have been, to quote from above, "the central and controlling motives of man's progress," and out of history as wonderfully and compactly told in them get a philosophy which at least for depth could not be surpassed. This deeper study, however, is not to be undertaken here. My work or our work at this time is to look directly to the facts of actual history, not to the organizing ideas of the philosophers, for illustration of its principles.

And just a word more may be said as to the method to be followed. In Part I, attention will be given to a careful analysis of several of the fundamental data of history, time, causation, nature, individuality, and progress; in Part II, to a study of society and of social evolution; and in Part III, to the consideration of such special problems in an understanding of history as the great man, the nature and function of evil, the conflict of the spiritual and the secular, and the origin and justification of revolution. And, finally, at the end will be undertaken the very dangerous and according to some—who may be right—the very inartistic labor of drawing a moral.

Part I.
DATA OF HISTORY.

CHAPTER I.

TIME.*

THAT time is one of the data of history goes without saying, and fully to comprehend history one must know just what time is. Is time an independent thing, external to the events or experiences that appear in it or is it in some way intrinsic to its content? Is it real in and of itself, even when empty, or, in such reality as it has, is it dependent on the nature of things, being when taken for itself only an abstraction of something that is directly and immediately involved in the very relations of things, or in what makes and determines the things themselves, or let us say in the activity that the relations of things presuppose? Is it, in short, a mere formal condition of history, or is it a material condition?

Now, unless time should prove to be something wholly by itself and wholly formal, real even when empty and so quite external to

*This chapter has already been published in large part in *The Philosophical Review*, January, 1899.

events, to discuss it abstractly, as I am now proposing to do, is to engage in a process of vivisection, which is always injurious if not fatal. Moreover, in this chapter, time will be found to be dependent instead of self-existent or external or formal. In its existence, in its peculiar character and in its peculiar function it will be seen to be determined by the other data of history, and they by it. So at the start we may as well recognize the vivisection that we are engaged in, and with the recognition postpone any final conclusions until the data of history as a living whole can stand and move before us. But, for the present, upon just what grounds is the self-existence or the formal character of time to be denied?

Well, in the first place, it is to be remarked that our question as to whether time is self-existent or dependent, formal or material, is only a special case of the general inquiry, with which the thought of modern times has been long imbued, as to whether the one and the many, unity and differences, are or are not functions of each other. Are differences essential to unity or is unity an abstract something that is quite independent of the differences in whatever is unified? Of course in the conception of an organism we have the one and the many, unity and differences, presented to us as interdependent and interdetermining, but even in these days not everybody is willing to accept all the consequences of this conception. As regards time, then, it is only one of the ways or media through which differences are unified. It is, to be sure, an extremely physical form of unification, but herein is nothing to place it out of the category to which I have just now assigned it. Space is another so-called physical form of unification, and philosophy is still asking about it as about time and as about unity in senses much less physical, if it is external to or intrinsic to the things that it unifies. Our present problem, then, is no peculiar problem; it is not isolated; and to have seen it in its larger relations or in its general character will certainly be of some help in its solution.

But now to turn directly to the business of this chapter, suppose we consider the conclusions that would naturally spring from regarding time as self-existent or formal. Four conclusions, that all merge into one as they are understood, have seemed to me worthy of mention.

In the first place, if time is merely formal, all events in time are necessarily external to each other and a history of merely dated happenings, a history that makes no study of laws or of causes, or of an organizing process, is justified. Indeed, no other history than that of separate events with dates would be possible. Simply, to appeal at once to the general case, if you make the unity of things external to their differences, you are bound therewith to separate the things themselves; and, again, specifically, if you make time external to events, you turn history into nothing but a broken series. I say a broken series, for continuity even in the most physical sense would be undiscoverable. A self-existent, purely formal time, by taking continuity to itself, denies it to the mere content of time.

Secondly, if time is formal, the things in time are sudden. Here, quite evidently, we have but another way of viewing the isolation referred to in the foregoing paragraph. Nations, men, institutions, are to be thought of, as if rising up out of nothing and disappearing as suddenly as they come, and whatever is at any time is only exactly that particular thing which it is, being without any changing or adapting or differentiating power or nature to relate it to other things. No doubt we are sometimes given to living as if time were only a formal condition of life, but the result is to make the days pass without any achievement on our part, life for us being as empty as the time that merely contains it, and to make such changes as do occur the work of a brutal chance or a lawless miracle. And, similarly, in a formal time history is no record of achievement, but a record of only sudden happenings or miraculous interventions.

In other words, thirdly, if time is formal, the events in time are naturally and necessarily under the control of some wholly external and therefore of some wholly arbitrary agency. To a people, for example, subject to some absolute monarch or to some infallible church, where monarch or church get their authority from a world or a nature altogether alien to this world and to human nature, time is a mere form, the present having no significance and the past and the future being unreal just because past and future.* What wonder that

*When time is self-existent and formal the present is only the absolute durationless now, the past is the wholly gone and the future simply and only that which has not yet come. See also my *Dynamic Idealism*, ch. xii: "Time."

through the middle ages the things of time were said to be illusory and predictions of the millenium were very common and the real or the spiritual was made altogether opposed to the temporal!

But, fourthly, in the illusory character of time, that necessarily follows from making it formal or external or self-existent, lies perhaps the most serious, the most thoroughly condemning conclusion of any that have been mentioned. Of course the isolation of events from each other, the sanction of chance or miracle, and the positive recognition of a controlling agency without are condemnatory enough, but for my own part I find the notion of time, or of anything else for that matter, as an illusion peculiarly offensive. The other conclusions stood for the moment without question, but here the need of a radically different view of time is absolutely imperative. To find an illusion is hopelessly to unsettle the point of view from which it is found and to enforce adoption of another point of view. *Summarily, if time is ever an experience, then the real and even the spiritual must be temporal.* But the real or the spiritual, you remind me, must be eternal. Very true, and in consequence there must be a sense in which the temporal and the eternal are not mere opposites, or mere negatives, of each other. And can we not find this sense? Can we not bring eternal spirit into the temporal? Can we not find in time, not something that is self-existent, for the self-existence ends in time as an illusion, but something that will show time to be only an abstraction of some *essential* character in the sphere of the real?

To make time *essential* to the real is to relate events positively or originally, to do away with all sudden beginnings and endings, to find the control of changes not in an external and therefore arbitrary agency but in the actual nature of that which is controlled, in an indwelling and only self-realizing process of things, and above all to make both the past and the future actual in the present and at one with it. Obviously a self-controlling process, a process that has its own determinations within itself, within its own conditions, can manifest only such differences as are organically, that is to say concretely related, and it can have only such a past and such a future as are, not external to the present, and so illusions, but actual contents of the present. A self-controlling process at every moment of its expression must both recapitulate its past and anticipate its future.

What the foregoing means must be found, at least in part, in that to which it is antithetical. Negatives always afford important help in interpretation. Still a direct or positive statement always needs more than mere statement. So, just what are related events? What is involved in the elimination of sudden changes? How can control be from within? And what is it to have past and future also present? These questions I can answer only preliminarily in this place, but I may turn my present labor into a pertinent illustration and say that I can not but hope that the explanations to be given here will have in themselves, as something not altogether intangible and unintelligible, the future that subsequent pages are to define more fully.

Thus, related events, which are of course sequent, are in principle like the successive experiences that one has when taking a walk. The stages of one's progress, whether future or past, are always present in the form of actual relations to the sphere of the activity. The walking is somehow only the temporal expression of spatial relations or the fulfilment of coexistences in sequences or of sequences in coexistences, and this expression or fulfilment would be impossible, were there not an actual and complete organic unity in all the differences involved. The action, I say, or the walking can be but the realization of already existing and ever existing relationships. Were the relationships that are expressed not rooted in some permanent organizing unity, were they not existing and persistent, it is hard to see, nay, it is impossible to see how the activity could ever come about or how the agent of it could ever know what he was doing. Merely that he may know what he is doing an agent needs an environment as a sphere of *coexisting* things or objects in whose relations he has repeated to him the past moments of his progress and foretold the future moments.

And in the circumstances of our illustration we see also what is meant by the elimination of sudden changes. The peculiar relation between the sequent and the coexistent that the conditions of activity evidently require makes continuity, as that alone in which the two can be at one with each other, a necessity. Indeed continuity is only a purely physical conception of relationship. Here we do well to broaden our view by thinking of the long process of evolution, which is not essentially different from that of walking. The larger facts of evolution will help us to a still clearer conception both of the relationship of events and of the continuity of change. Evolution has outcome not only in a creature that has "evolved" but also in a vitally related environment by which the creature's past and the creature's future are made concretely present. Moreover a consciousness of the environment is as necessary a condition of the evolutional process as was the pedestrian's recognition of his surroundings a necessary condition of his progress. Evolution needs consciousness, and consciousness, in our larger illustration as in our smaller, means both a relational unity of coexistences and a continuity of sequences.

Also in the primary importance of consciousness to evolution there is to be had still another view of what now interests us. In a word, life and consciousness can not possibly be thought of as apart from each other. Consciousness, then, is as original as life, and in their common origin or, as the same thing, in their constant contemporaneity is evidence of their unity. Life, because it is life, is conscious. Consciousness is intrinsic to life; it is not under any conditions epiphenomenal. To make consciousness a sudden appearance in the evolution-series is to separate it always from the life to which it is attached. Some scientists, whose eyes must be closed to their own visions, seem to enjoy the strange conceit that science, as the best expression of man's consciousness, is solely for science's sake, and the same blind gazers, as if unwittingly correcting their unseen error, have been wont to raise animals to man's level by making the animal consciousness also epiphenomenal or for its own sake, and to raise the still "lower" forms of life to the animal's level by denying consciousness to them altogether; but the very evolution which they unwittingly justify would be impossible on their scheme. Evolution demands a consciousness or if you will a science or a thought or a mind that is *intimate* with the nature of whatever evolves.

But time as the form in which the sequences of evolution appear is a peculiar condition of consciousness, so that in identifying life and consciousness we do in just so far make time essential to reality. True, somebody is likely to turn upon us and declare that life itself is not essential, that life began in time by some process of abiogenesis or spontaneous genesis and is not an ultimate fact in the reality of the present and that time therefore is not of such a nature as to make the temporal and the eternal one, but to such an objector, it is only necessary to reply that he means less by life than we do. For us the life that can evolve is not the special endowment of an isolated body or of a group, large or small, of isolated bodies; it is a property of the universe as single and indivisible;* and with life so established and conscious in and of itself the idea of time as essential to reality is unassailable.

Life, or action, in its temporal sequences is but the continuous expression of the persistent relationships of coexistences. This is a formula that is, confessedly, not pleasant, but it is quite intelligible to all who walk and to all also who, knowing the story of their evolution, look out upon their present environment, which is so obviously at once the recapitulated but contemporized past and the anticipated but con-

*In subsequent pages special attention is to be given to the view of life that is here only asserted. See the chapter on "Individuality."

temporized future. And that life under this formula is self-determined goes now without saying. Simply there is no creation to make determination from without necessary. There is neither an external past nor an external future to act upon the present and make it helpless. But of the need, involved in making time essential to reality, of finding past and future actual in the relations of the present, more may be said. Perhaps we are not accustomed to look upon a creature's environment* as its past and future organically contemporized with the present, but in other ways we are at least indirectly familiar with the idea. Memories are recognized as states of mind that are to be referred to *present* organically related physiological processes, and the same is true of prophecies. Also as evolutionists or historians we are wont to explain the past or the future by appealing to principles that we look upon as independent of any of the distinctions of time. Evolutionists to-day are relying in so many ways on mechanics, on chemistry, on physics, which in so far as "exact" sciences are also timeless sciences;

---

*It does not seem necessary for me to say here that as I use the term environment I would have it all-inclusive. Obviously a creature's own body is a part of its environment.

and historians use nature and nature's laws in their accounts of human achievement and progress. That laws, however, or principles are always contemporizing agencies, bringing the past and the future to which they are applied into the present, is all but axiomatic. Thus are we brought back to the view of environment already given, since environment is not only the sphere of life's coexisting conditions but also, as an object of consciousness, the very incarnation of a more or less clearly recognized law. In a formula, environment is only the actuality, and one might almost say, the substantiality of life's contemporizing law. The biological doctrine of recapitulation, if taken for what it is in reality, a doctrine of a lawful environment as well as of the organic unity of an individual creature, offers us a very good concluding indication of what is meant by time as essential to reality or by any of the consequences of the essence-theory of time, by the relation of events, the continuity of change, the indwelling nature of control or determination, and the contemporaneity of past and future with the present.

And now again the question, with which this chapter began: What is time? Plainly time is nothing in itself. An abstract definition of it, however, may be derived from the foregoing, although I should almost prefer to let what has been said stand as it is without this addition. Time in and for itself alone, time as mere duration, is definable as a physical or quantitative abstraction for organic unity in so far as organic unity involves change; or, differently and somewhat metaphorically put, it is the change that is inherent in the organic, projected upon the plane of mere measurable quantity. Similarly, space is the permanence of the organic on the same plane. But, in a statement that is possibly a shade less abstruse, time is an element in experience that expresses abstractly at once the necessity—the past—and the opportunity—the future—that a world of related differences naturally affords. Time, then, is no mere form of life, self-existent and external; it is even a force, or it is a phase of a force, in application of which or in identification with which life consists. Those who live do not live *in* time; they live time itself, they use time; and a life that uses time is as eternal as it is temporal.*

* Possibly I have made a mistake in almost assuming in this chapter that the organic and the real are literally synonymous terms. One has to assume something, however, and in another book, already referred to, *Dynamic Idealism*, I have considered at length the organic nature of reality. "Relationship among things is the criterion neither of a life nor of a mind that exists apart from the substance of the universe. It is, however, the criterion of substance itself, and as the central truth about things it bears this witness: *The universe itself lives; the universe itself thinks.*"

CHAPTER II.

CAUSATION.

AS a matter of form I may begin this second chapter by saying that our idea of causation, the second datum of history to occupy us, has already been determined by the idea of time to which we are now committed; and this, although as has been suggested each new study that we enter upon can not but react upon all that precedes and give to it a deeper as well as a clearer meaning.

Heat expands. Columbus discovered America. The University of Michigan was founded by an act of 1837. The earth revolves about the sun. Here are a number of statements of causal relationship that in various ways illustrate what we have now to explain. Every one of them, at least as commonly understood, amounts to an assertion that some individual force or agency, as an antecedent in time, has in and of itself, produced some subsequent specific or individual change in the order of things. Even in the last of the four cases, which is the case that might be most in doubt, the sun is very likely to to be regarded as a body that individually controls the earth's movement; or, if not the sun, then some other great central body, indefinitely remote, to whose force the solar system as a whole is made subject.

But causation, if individualistic, temporally sequent, and arbitrarily productive or creative, is a conception that involves very serious objections. In fact the objections are so serious that upon being properly indicated they condemn the conception itself absolutely.

Any individual that is in itself a cause of something other than itself can not but be viewed as itself the effect of some other cause, while that which it has effected must in its turn be a cause of something not itself. In other words, whatever is externally or arbitrarily productive is also externally or arbitrarily produced; and, conversely, whatever is externally or arbitrarily produced is also externally or arbitrarily productive. Thus, in the sense already pointed out, we can never say that heat expands or that the University was founded in 1837 or in general that a causes b

without at once forcing attention upon an indefinite, nay, an infinite series of causes and an infinite series of effects. But strangely enough, unless it is not strange but natural that errors should eventually correct themselves, either one of the two series amounts to nothing more or less in the end than the universe as a whole to which the first observed cause and its assigned effect alike belong. Moreover, whenever in practice the two series, that are also identical, are presented to thought, the ultimate cause and the ultimate effect, although perhaps regarded as separate individual existences, are always conceived in terms of a nature or principle that is altogether independent of either spatial or temporal limitations. The first cause and the last effect are always, each of them, only the inner nature or the inner law that the two series have manifested. They are at once terms in the series and all-including summaries of the series. To give a very simple illustration, in childhood, youth, manhood, and old age, there is presented a series, which has for both its first and its last terms, *as we conceive them ordinarily*, rather a conception of human nature in the abstract than anything else.

The child as father of the man is the man not yet defined, the principle from whose expression the mature man is to spring, and old age is but a defined manhood returning to the spirit of its childhood. Both childhood and old age show human nature at one with itself, and to either of them we may look, not for mere terms in the series, but for the principle or the spirit, independent of distinctions of place and time, that controls because including the whole series. But this curious, yet natural, outcome of the notion that causation is individualistic reduces any statement of casual relationship to the simple if not empty formula that the whole is the cause of itself or that a real cause and its real effect are identical. Therefore, whatever else may be implied, causation is not individualistic.

Of course the individual, that is at once arbitrarily productive and arbitrarily produced, is only the isolated and sudden event of the previous chapter in different clothes and the conclusion about causation that our very simple criticism has just brought us to is equivalent exactly to our organic contemporization of the past and the future with the present. Then we spoke from the standpoint of time; now, as if the two were separable, from the standpoint of time's content. But, clearly, to identify cause and effect is to contemporize past and future.

And another equally interesting way of reaching the same result is to regard directly and specifically the objection to ever identifying a mere temporal antecedent with a cause or a mere temporal consequent with an effect. A time interval, however short, between a cause and its effect is fatal alike to one's idea of time and to one's idea of causation. Not to repeat what has been said already, the interval can never be anything but a source of possible if not necessary change or disturbance. An antecedent cause can not be fully responsible for its effect. A subsequent effect can not be the real effect of its cause. Here we have, as it were, a criticism that is intensive in its view instead of extensive. Instead of looking to the larger whole to which any cause and its effect must belong, we are now looking to what a cause and its effect within their own sphere and through their own time must include. A cause, then, that deserts its process for however short an interval, can not be sure of fulfilment, or whatever results from it can be referred to it only if it is "abstractly conceived," as Spinoza would say, that is, confusedly identified with all the intervening influences as making one continuous process. A pistol-shot, for example, may and it may not kill a man, but if cause and effect are really separate in time, any treatment of the wound would be at best only a game of chance if not absolutely aimless and idle. Indeed, to express the case at its extreme, there would be quite as much reason for anyone who heard a pistol fired to drop dead on the spot as to do something for his self-preservation. Whether he were hit or not would be an impertinent consideration. In practical life, however, we cannot desert for a single moment what we are doing without damaging our achievement and we certainly can not suppose, as so often we seem to, that nature is less a servant of her tasks than we are of ours. True, every cause has an effect, every effect a cause, but a cause is nothing more nor less than an activity and its effect is only the manifested conditions of this activity. Most assuredly a wounded man is not dead until he is dead and he lives just as long as he is alive. Do excuse my positive inanity here, remembering that the fault is not wholly mine, so long as others of my race, at least in their minds, insist on actually killing their fellows before they are dead or—as the same thing in principle—making them live sometimes as if after and sometimes as if before their actual life-time. Obviously I have now left such cases of death as those from pistol-shots and taken a more general view. Deaths and births are interests of historians—as well as of doctors and relatives. To make a, an antecedent, the cause of b, a consequent, is only the general case under which falls, as special and particular, the still common habit of either condemning or praising men who lived and died years or centuries ago as if they were responsible to life as it is known today or as if they were even behind instead of ahead of their own times. It would be safe for historians, for the sake of their history, to remember that men, never being isolated creatures, never can be either behind their times or ahead of their times. Time and its content are one, not two. Both the history and the biology of today, not always directly but very often indirectly, are given to the offense, the anachronism, of separating cause and effect in time, and it suffices to say that just as long as they offend in this way they are making the processes, which concern them, lawless, irresponsible processes, the study of which can bear no fruit.

That a temporally antecedent cause is always an isolated individual is an axiom—may I not now call it that?—which may help to give unity to the criticisms that have been made so far, but before taking another step an accusation that may be brought by somebody must be met. Perhaps I seem to have been contradicting myself. Thus, at one moment I seem to have insisted on dispensing with the distinction of time and at the next to have objected strenuously to any such thing, and this appears seriously contradictory. The *organic* contemporization, however, of past and future with present, for which I have been contending, has always been for the integrity of historical order, not for its overthrow. No antecedent is cause apart from its whole environment and relating it to its whole environment is exactly what effects its contemporization with its effect. Not Columbus, in 1492, discovered America, but Columbus aided by the trade-winds and other natural agencies of

1899; or, again, in 1492 Columbus discovered not the America of today but an America that was only the "other world," which had become more than a mere spiritual dream in Europe even before the ships sailed. The famous voyage had only its own motive for its immediate result; the result was no more and no less than its motive. It became more, but that is another story. So, returning, I say that my apparent contradiction was only apparent. The past and the future are relations, or related parts, of the present; they are not external causes, they are not external effects.

Thirdly, to object to an individualistic and temporally sequent causation because it is also creational is to be only just a little bit more commonplace than I have been already. Commonplaces, however, are the business of philosophy. In addition, then, to what has been said above, causation even ceases to be causation if it is arbitrary; the effect of any cause is so idle or so useless to the cause itself, being as unmeaning as stones to a man asking for bread or antiquities to speculators in stocks. Modern science, so keenly interested in a lawful nature, has been established, it is true, upon the familiar principles of universal causation and the uniformity of nature; but the effect of the universality and uniformity, which the principles assert, has been to reduce causation itself as a relation between two things to a mere formality of sequence or coexistence. For science causation has become rather a form of thought than anything discovered or discoverable in the objective world. A lawful nature, dependent on uniformity and universality, on conservation and indivisibility, has forbidden anything even distantly suggestive of creation.

But, if causation is not to be thought of as individualistic, temporally sequent, and creational, what can we say of it? We must come to some definite understanding of its nature, if for no other reason, at least for the sake of a comprehension of history, in which it has such an important part. True, a causation, which puts the control of a process outside of the process itself or—in words amounting to essentially the same thing—which identifies cause and effect with temporal antecedent and temporal consequent, is offensive to thought; but how else can the manifold changes of the world be adequately explained? Merely to conclude that cause and effect are contemporary and materially identical is anything but satisfactory.

Causation, the causal relationship, as is shown by the use that modern science has made of it, is only one of the ways in which we present to ourselves the unity of the world. Accordingly, when we identify it with the world's change or differentiation, our conception of it must depend upon whether in general we think of unity and differences as mutually exclusive or as intrinsic to each other. If unity and differences exclude each other, then causation is just that to which we have been objecting so positively, but if, as we believe, they involve each other, if they are perfect functions of each other, then causation is nothing more nor less than organic differentiation. In organic differentiation the whole always is the cause of itself, the positive causation consisting only in the consistent or responsible expression of the organic relations or in the interaction of parts that the organic nature implies. For brevity's sake, then, I shall hereafter refer to causation in this sense as responsible or relational in distinction from an arbitrary or creational causation.

Now exactly what our relational or responsible causation amounts to can be seen in part at least by reflection upon such simple cases of change or differentiation as travel and motion.* Travel is most decidedly something more than leaving places and visiting places; it is the expression of already existing and never ceasing relations, the fulfilment and maintenance of developed interests. And it is this so truly that we are able to say, in spite of the paradoxes, that a traveller always is at his goal even when he starts, his future as a developed relation or interest being concretely present, and at his starting point even when he arrives, his past also being concretely present. If we think of travel in any other way we forget—do we not?—what we are. Only travellers can travel; only creatures of manifold interests or relations can ever express the differentiation of a journey; and creatures that have such interests travel in spite of themselves. Any organism, for example, is born to travel, for the simple reason that it can not leave home behind and yet must ever be visiting new places. In practical life some seem

* Of these I have already written at some length in *Dynamic Idealism* (see Ch. II. "Change."), but a little repetition can hardly do any harm—especially in the light of modern psychology, which makes repetition impossible!

to travel without having any previous relation to the places they visit and some to lose their old relations when they leave their homes, but the seeming is only a seeming. A fellow-countryman once slapped me on the shoulder in the streets of Berlin and relying on my American patriotism walked with me for several blocks. He was rejoiced to meet me and he told me of his very extensive wanderings. "Regardless of cost" he had gone "from Rome through Florence to Venice and way stations," and so on, and each place that he visited had or had not "met his expectations." That was his formula and his experiences began and ended with it, so that I wondered what could have brought him so many miles from home. His money? Certainly nothing else seemed to relate him in any real way to what he had come to. His money and his formula were the sole motives of his travel, since they alone kept him at home even in his absence, for I must say again that the traveller can express in his journey only the relations that he has, never entering a strange place nor leaving a familiar one.

And what is true of travel is true of motion. We think of motion as the expression of a continuous series of positions, but just because it is this it is also just a little more than this. Any position in the series involves all the others, or is itself real only through its relation to the others, so that the motion instead of being a mere succession or even a continuous succession of positions is the expression or realization of a system of relations. Accordingly things do not move, that is to say, motion is not peculiar to things as' such, as any one who has reflected at all on the relativity of motion has realized, but motion is the relations of things in expression.

Change of any sort, finally, is of the same character. As much the motive as the end, as much the condition as the result of a life that is essentially organic, it can never be anything else but the expression of existing relationship. Not nature as a whole changes; not the parts as mere parts change, nor do they of themselves produce changes without, but the change in nature is the interaction of her different parts in fulfilment of the organic whole.

"Heat expands," then, is a formula, which we can now interpret only as meaning that heat, instead of being a peculiar force acting upon external conditions and producing in them what we know as expansion, is a force that has expansion as one of its forms. Expansion is a special condition of heat, or it is one of the many organically related mutations of heat. The simple doctrine of the mutability of forces is in its own rather indirect way an assertion of just what has here been meant by a relational or responsible causation.

And, even again to refer to Columbus, in his discovery of America he owed much to the winds and currents, and his journey resulted only in the fulfilment of its motive. Europe had come to have too realistic a faith in another world, even in the present reality of another world, she believed too strongly that the other world was near at hand, to make the change to the consciousness of America across the seas seem anything but an experience for which there had been an adequate preparation. Columbus' journey was just like other journeys, the fulfilment of developed interests. Historians, thinking of his caravels and their westward course, should remember that America came into European life, just as Christianity came to Mediterranean life, only when the times were ripe for it.

Furthermore, as regards the third case, it is a simple truth, evident to any one, that laws and ordinances only define existing conditions; they are never creative. The University of Michigan existed in fact, it existed as a condition, before the defining or constituting act was passed. Certainly the University had as much to do with creating the act as the act with creating the University. Similarly the American constitution, in spite of the social-contract theory that prevailed when our constitution was formulated, is not and was not creative, but only definitive of the social life over which it has authority. Nor, obviously enough, did man's discovery of the little formula, $v = gt$, introduce into the world the interesting phenomenon of falling bodies.

And as for the earth's revolution about the sun, it suffices to say that the law of gravity or rather the inner organic nature defined by the law is the true controlling centre—clearly not a spatially fixed centre—of the system. With a formal time and with an arbitrary causation we should have to think of the system as moving off into some unknown and, what is worse, into some essentially unknowable realm. The movement would be nothing but unrest, displacement, without existing relation to any goal; and the system's future would be comparable exactly with that of a man who had to walk forward without anything to walk towards. But walking, that has a goal, presupposes a *contemporary* relation to the future, and the music of the heavenly spheres has the same presupposition.

Causation, then, in the light of our criticisms and illustrations, is—as already described—organic differentiation, that is to say, the consistent or responsible expression of an organic unity or the interaction of the related parts of an indivisible and persisting self-asserting whole*. If reality is organic, unity and difference being essential to each other, no other conception of change is necessary than this that makes it consist in the permanence, the expression and maintenance, of that which is. Still our notion of change and causation must be lacking in clearness until we have explicitly defined to ourselves the character and function of individuality.

* Other definitions of causation, already given implicitly if not explicitly, are such as these: "Organic contemporization of past and future with present"; "manifestation of the conditions of activity"; "unification"; "responsible or relational activity"; and so on.

CHAPTER III.

NATURE.

BEFORE inquiring directly into the character and function of individuality it will be well worth while to extract from the foregoing the view of nature that has been involved.

Nature is a term peculiarly ambiguous but other possible meanings of it aside the meaning here has reference to nature as the sphere of man's activity or for that matter of the activity of any living creature. Nature here means environment. It means the outer world. It means the larger including life to which we and so many others in some way belong. And in this sense it has been an important datum of history.

But a very definite conception of the relation of living creatures, or human creatures, to nature has been between the lines of the conclusions which have been reached about time and about causation. Briefly, then, to begin with, if time is not a formal but a material condition of activity, of history or evolution, and if causation is not arbitrary but responsible, then nature and man, or let us say in general the sphere of life and life itself are very intimately related. In fact the relation to nature is so intimate that at least for man it is even a *personal* relation. This may seem to be a suggestion for the philosophy of religion rather than for the philosophy of history, but in my own view it has as fitting a place here as anywhere. Still let the word itself go, if it is confusing to anybody. In any case, of the positive intimacy of the relation there can be no doubt.

A formal time both gives a broken history, or broken evolution, and separates the present phases of life from each other, and an arbitrary causation both means an original creation, or a succession of creations, and makes present activities dependent on purely arbitrary or external determinations. For a scheme of thought, then, which admits a formal time and an arbitrary causation, nature can be only a general term for something that was, before human life or any sort of life began, and that ever since has been a source of external determination, or at least a something, adjustment to which requires superhuman or superanimate power. Accordingly, from such a standpoint history can be only a struggle against unfair conditions, a contest with what is absolutely alien and unsympathetic; and both progress and retrogression, whenever either is seen to have taken place, can be explained only by the assumption of some interference, good or evil, from without. Of course the recognition of such interference may bring unity into what would be chaos without it, but it certainly casts a fatal shadow over the view that makes it necessary.

With time and causation in character as we have found them nature appears at once as the helpful mediator of man's activity, ever present to hold him up in his struggle, not with her as an alien and brutal force, but with himself as directly and fully responsible to her. Nature as outwardly present to him is only the environment in which we have found past and future contemporized with the present; not something that was, before he was, and still remains as far from him as before he came, but something that holds him in and with herself as a mother her child.

So conceived a life with nature, however difficult the struggle, however sharp the tension of the manifold relations or responsibilities, is in need of—or should I not say is in danger of?—no interference from without. It induces its own determinations. It is free, that is to say, it is life, because the necessities are its own necessities.

But somebody here reminds me that man has a spiritual nature as well as a physical, that he is intimately related to the spiritual as well as to the natural. This is perfectly true and, curiously enough, it is exactly what I mean, exactly what I am trying to show. Man, not something apart from him, has indeed a spiritual nature. The natural man and the spiritual man—are they two or only one? If two, then our study so far has been altogether idle. For us, to translate our conclusions into these new terms, the spiritual can be but the expression of the natural or physical; it can not possibly be escape from the natural or from the physical.

Of course in changing our ideas of cause and time we have also changed our ideas of nature and matter and this should not be lost sight of, for a nature that can be man's helpful mediator is a new, a transfigured nature. Its face, perhaps, is too new and too bright for any whose minds are still possessed with the tenets of materialism or of materialism's natural counterpart, spiritualism; but herein is no reason for refusing to look upon it.

CHAPTER IV.

INDIVIDUALITY.

FOR a comprehensive philosophy of history the individual must be something besides what we ordinarily understand by a person, and this means simply, among other things, that personality itself must be *in principle* something more extensive than our usual application of the term would indicate. Indeed, the usual application of any term is never adequate to its inner meaning. Individuality, then, really involves animals as well as persons and things as well as animals. All creatures are individuals. Things said to be living and things said to be dead are individuals. Molecules and atoms are individuals. And what is an individual?

The views of individuality, I can hardly say the possible views, since only one view can be possible, but the views that need here to be considered, are two; and, as might be expected, they belong to the two schemes of thought, each to its own, that have been treated and set over against each other in all of the preceding chapters. Thus, either individuality is a matter of endowment or indwelling nature and power, or it is a matter of function, of organic function. But which of the two can it be?

The endowment theory of the individual, which almost at once will be seen to belong to the system of thought that would have time formal and causation arbitrary, is a theory that makes force and life and consciousness and will the peculiar indwelling properties of that to which they are assigned. To express force, as in the case of an atom or a molecule, or of any peculiar manifestation in nature, of clouds, say, or of winds, or of stones, or of heavenly bodies, is to act occultly, to act upon what is in no sense a condition of the activity. To live is to have relation to what is lifeless, as in the case of an organism adapting itself to essentially inorganic conditions; it is to be subject to what may fairly be called a biological creed that sees life only under some preconceived and unchanging and unchangeable form. Witness the conception of immutable species or of caste in nature, or of eternal election and damnation, conceptions from no one of which modern life, although perhaps generally literally free, can be said to be spiritually so. To be conscious is to apprehend something with which the conscious being has nothing to do, consciousness—whether of self or of what is without, of the not-self—if an indwelling endowment being of necessity only epiphenomenal. Thus, it is a consciousness whose sensations comprise but material elements—fixed in nature and value and so "given"—of thought, and whose thoughts or inner states are but the arbitrary unifying forms that receive the sensuous material as only so much gratuitously profered content, and that are themselves as fixed and as gratuitous as what they receive; a consciousness, then, that at one moment may seem to justify the doctrines of the English sensationalists, and at the next those of the French and German Nativists and Rationalists. To have will, or volition, is to act irresponsibly or creatively or, if I may repeat a term already used, to act *occultly*. And, finally, to have force, and life, and consciousness, and volition, is to be four distinctly separate individuals all in one. Moreover, and this is the striking fact, the endowment theory of individuality never finds and never can find an individual in its universe that is not, to all intents and purposes, all four in one.

How can this be? Why, to consider only two of the several cases, to live on the endowment plan, not only as a matter of doctrine but also as a matter of practice, is to make the external conditions of life, that are supposed to be lifeless, alive *on the same plan*; or, putting the same truth differently, on the endowment plan the individual is not alive in and of itself, so that anything, particularly anything that is a recognized condition of life, can live and in fact must live in the same external or beside-itself way. Also, secondly, in the case of consciousness, the object of conscious is just as conscious as the subject. Objects are conscious, *epiphenomenally* conscious, in what we are pleased to call their physical or only sensible qualities. Berkeley was right enough in finding nothing in a physical quality but a sensation, and Schopenhauer, among others, in turning Kant's transcendentalism, or phenomenalism, into pessimism and voluntarism. But, says somebody, it is supremely absurd to say that objects are conscious. Perhaps it is, but in the first place I am not trying to avoid absurdities, only to draw conclusions, and in the second place it is also true that on the endowment plan subjects are in and of themselves as unconscious as objects. An epiphenomenal consciousness is no better than unconsciousness; nay, it is unconsciousness. So to be epiphenomenally conscious is to be nothing more nor less than an unconscious physical thing with sensible qualities, and *vice versa*. And, further, for I will touch very briefly upon another case, the will of what the endowment theory regards a moral or responsible being can not be in any respect different from the indwelling force of a lifeless, unconscious, non-moral, physical thing. Hereafter, in illustration of this truth, we shall see that in history the notion of will or executive authority as getting its sanction from another sphere than that in which the expression or execution takes place, or in other words as being mediate instead of immediate, or given instead of inherent, has always meant in practice that might, strictly physical might, brute force, makes right. Names, it is important for us to keep in mind constantly, do not necessarily differentiate things. What history at one time chose to call the spiritual was the physical also.

So, in its important consequences, the endowment theory of the individual is now before us. Is it possible? Can we think it? No; and just because, when made at all reflective or self-conscious, it can not even think itself. As if before our very eyes, it has already passed out of itself. The necessity, which we have discovered in it, of recognizing all individuals in every individual, the conscious in the unconscious, the voluntary in the dynamic, the lifeless in the living, and so on, has revealed to us a theory—none other than the organic function theory—which must find in life and consciousness and will and force only so many characters or principles that are all of them, first, intimately or *essentially* involved in each other and, secondly, not peculiar and localized endowments, *but affairs of the universe as an indivisible whole.*

Now this second theory is far from asserting that stones are conscious voluntary beings or that clods live. It asserts only, what was as true to the endowment theory as to it, that stones are as conscious and as voluntary as any other bodies, even as your body or as mine, and that clods are as animate as any other physical masses, even as protoplasm or still more specifically as biophores, and then in such assertions it sees, concealed perhaps but still present and actual, another view—its own view—of life and consciousness. Life and consciousness, and also will and force, as affairs of an indivisible universe, are—what can we say?—only principles of organization or differentiation. Consciousness is the tension of organic relationship, or of organic differentiation; life, a name for the activity that such relationship or differentiation involves; and will or force, the activity itself in the light of the tension. Stones, or any objects, are accordingly conscious only in the sense of being positive conditions of consciousness, and clods live only as equally positive, which is to say, essentially vital conditions of life.

And precisely what is the individual in a universe that, although possessing life and consciousness and force and will, refuses to be divided? Clearly it can be no separate entity, whether atom or biophore or person, with never mind how many separate indwelling endowments. What then? An organic function—which is obviously a tautology; a relation—which may seem an idle abstraction to some but which is, to say the least, as real, as concrete and palpable, as any endowed entity ever was; or, finally, a responsible activity—which may sound sensational, or sentimental, but which is not absurd necessarily. Remember, we are indeed interested primarily in a philosophy of the history of mankind, but any mere sentiments that this interest may excite are quickly subdued with our duty to the individuality of atoms as well as of men, of things as well as of persons. Only the view, that takes heed of the universe, can ever be worth our while.

Our individual, then, is an organic function. The cell, the hand or eye, the laborer in a factory where division of labor is expressed—and in some measure it always is expressed, the social leader of any sort—and every individual leads in something, the pianist, whether as one man among others or as an activity that is in relation to life as a whole, or any animal, whose life in any way serves its environment as well as itself, is an organic function.

And, perhaps more generally, the individual is a relation. Relationship, however, is exactly what organic function means, so that the examples above are as apt here as there. But also the point is a relation, being that through which, so to speak, the conception of the organic entered into the history of mathematics or through which pure mechanics, finding motion in a line and force in the motion, came to light. The atom, as only a centre of force, is a relation, and, so viewed, has made the idea of mutability of forces, an idea which is as biological as physical, a possible idea. The star, or the planet, is a relation; else the law of gravitation would be a myth.

But the individual is a responsible activity. In this third account the two others are fully united or identified. Relationship, if real or actual, is inevitable responsibility, and a responsible activity can not be anything else but an organic function. Here, with the examples already given, may be mentioned the members of the family, the father, the mother, the child.

Evidently the great difference between the endowment theory and the organic function theory is just this. The former completely separates the individual and his activity: the latter completely identifies them.

How do individuals arise? This, under a view that can recognize only a relational or responsible in place of an arbitrary causation and only a material in place of a formal time is not a pertinent question. For our present standpoint there is no question of mere origin just as there is and can be no question of mere destiny. Individuals neither come to be nor cease to be. They are and they are ever in expression. The expression, as always at once a differentiating and an organizing process, has the effect of focusing or centering individuals in forms that are spatially and temporally defined, but it does nothing more. A focused individual—I do not quite like the metaphor myself but I can find no better one—is only the specialized overt expression of an activity that is as inclusive as the universe itself. The specialization, of course, is due to the tension or the consciousness, *being both a condition and a result of it*, which is inherent in the organic whole. Thus, handling, as an activity, without being any less actual or concrete, is more general than hands, existing before the development of hands and being now more extensive than the hands that are; and fatherhood and motherhood are more general or more extensive, both temporally and spatially, than fathers and mothers; and cell-formation than cells, leadership than leaders, music than pianists, hammering than hammers, thought than thinkers, motion than positions or points, force than forces. Not by any means that the more general and the centred or focused individual are in any sense two, nor that the consciousness of the one, in the sense of consciousness as a tension of organic relationship, is not also the consciousness of the other,—that plainly is not my meaning, but simply that the focusing, the differentiation, makes the consciousness clearer and determines more precisely the individual's place in the whole.

Is this a new idea of individuality? Hardly. If it were really new it would not be possible; we could not think it. With what is possible, with what is true, we are always more familiar than we ever know. Thus with this idea of the individual as not some thing apart from activity but as itself an organic function, in which the agent and the act are one and the same thing, the thought of today must find itself, nay, is finding itself surprisingly well acquainted. In almost countless ways, that are not always reflected upon, it is identifying instead of separating individuals and their activity. It is finding an identity between what lives and life itself, between what wills and the deeds willed, between what thinks and what is thought, and between what exerts force and force itself. Do I need to give examples? Here are a few. The thought of today is explaining men by their time; referring acts in general to their conditions—instead of to some external will originally good or originally bad; taking, then, not the will for the deed but the deed for the will; insisting on proved capacity as the sole evidence of right to authority; in short, putting character—and let me say, character of atoms as well as of persons, for physics is not behind ethics or politics—above mere position. No longer are endowed rights or powers allowed to positions of any kind. Positions, everywhere, are relations.

Here is a tool, a pocket-knife, the means to somebody's activity; and are the agent and the act and the tool to be treated as three things, or two, or only one? They can hardly be more than one. Of course the agent is more than a mere whittler, but also his act is more than mere whittling, and the knife itself, in which are embodied the very principles of all tools, is more than a mere knife, so that, although we see the three as different, we do so only by seeing the agent, for example, and the knife or the act and the knife or the agent and the act from different points of view, whereas such differences of view are not at all fair to the question that we asked. An act, in general, is often thought to be somebody's application of natural force to his own ends, and in this view the applying agent and the applied force and the mediating activity are not identified; but their separation is due to the conflicting points of view, as just shown. Surely, in the case of anybody's act, it is quite as true that nature applies her own force or that environment acts on itself as that the individual applies the force or acts on the environment. The application of any force is only the expression of force as such, which is to say, of all force.

Again, I cross my study to the thermometer to find what the temperature is. Here, besides activity, the fact of consciousness is involved. This was not absent before, only kept out of sight. Are my consciousness of the thermometer's record and the thermometer itself and the temperature of the room three things, or two, or only one? These also can be only one. The thermometer does but show nature, as it were, measuring herself, reacting upon herself, unless forsooth the expansion of the mercury is to be separated from the heat of the room. But, some one says, the measurement is my consciousness, not nature's, nature being unconscious. How can any one backslide in this way? Such a statement may suit the endowment theory, but it is impossible; it is positively wrong. The consciousness that takes me to the thermometer is as much the effect of the heat as the cause of my going, the going itself being only one of the many motions in which the heat of the room has found expression. The hot room, then, to which I belong, reacting on itself, or I as warm reacting on myself as a function of the room, which is my environment, is all that any one can get out of the process. It is all, I say, but that is a good deal. Through the tension of the reaction the process is a conscious one. I find out something. My experience, or my activity, which has its relation of course to a larger experience or a larger activity, becomes defined, and in one direction or the other I change the temperature of the room, opening the register or raising a window, or—with the same meaning—the room changes its own temperature. The definition of experience or activity is always followed by expression of the larger experience or the larger activity, and this, obviously enough, because the larger experience or activity is in the definition.

But what materialism! What determinism! Only, fortunately, names never condemn. But sometimes their application ends by transforming their meaning completely. In an earlier chapter I must have seemed materialistic or deterministic when I virtually denied to Columbus the discovery of America, finding in the voyage of the caravels only his discovery of himself or America's discovery of herself, but that and this are very different indeed from what most understand by those offensive names. The activity of an individual that expresses only what in its own nature it is responsible to, namely, its own relations or its own conditions, may be a determined activity, for responsibility implies determination, but the determination is immanent or essential, not external. It may, too, be a result of a "material" environment, but not unless with as much truth the "material" environment is also a result of it, the two being functionally related. Or, again, if environment's act is also the agent's act, then both materialism and determinism are transformed. By the deep experience which their application to activity upon this plan brings them they are converted; they are spiritually regenerated.

Individuals, as relations or organic functions or responsible activities, having their reality in and of what they do, in the very fact of their expression serve to define both the process to which they belong and their own positive part in it. Their very activity, their focusing, brings a completer organization and a clearer consciousness both to themselves and to the whole that includes them. Moreover, the consciousness that they define and the activity that they express are their consciousness and their activity. They have, in other words, a substantial, not a merely formal part in what goes on. At first thought it might seem as if under the organic function theory individuals, both in their consciousness and their activity, were hopelessly subjected to the including whole, but this is exactly what does not happen. The whole is not an including whole, but an organic whole. The consciousness and the activity, therefore, belong neither to the parts nor to the whole, in the sense of either to the exclusion of the other, but are among the parts or intrinsic to the relations of the parts, and so belong to the whole only through and in these relations. The consciousness of the parts is itself the consciousness of the whole and the activity of the parts is itself the activity of the whole. Under the organic function theory a conscious and responsible individuality is a necessity, being as original and as constantly active as unity or wholeness itself. As relations, as responsible activities, individuals have an inalienable reality.

We have, then, an individuality that transcends any mere bounds of space and time without in any way relieving us of a direct duty to what now is and is now involving us. The endowment theory implied such a transcendence too, but only by virtually removing all present and manifest relationships. Endowment itself was transcendence, but it was also isolation from all the conditions of action and so even from self. Here, however, in the individual as an organic function, we have transcendence without alienation or isolation. The individual, instead of being spatially and temporally determined on the one hand and spiritually or immaterially real and immortal on the other, is real and immortal just because a spatial and temporal individual. Of course, in this case the meanings of space and time are changed. The spatial and temporal individual, being in and of itself more than a local and momentary existence, requires no other separate part in which to secure for itself a permanent reality. Is fatherhood or motherhood born? Or does it die? Do any of the relations of life, identification with which is just that upon which a real individuality depends, either come into being or pass away? Some time ago, in observing that the individual is never a new activity, but only a general activity focused, or a force in particular relation or application, we saw that individuals were not born, and it is equally true that they do not pass away. Individual expression and individual consciousness define; they do not create, they do not destroy. Handling, for example, not only precedes but it also survives hands; and so of seeing in relation to eyes, of hammering to hammers, of kingship to kings, of monetary exchange to money, and of any individual activity, more simple or more complex, to the things or organs with which we identify it. In fine, identify an individual with its activity, seeing in its life and consciousness and will and force an actual relationship, a real organic function, and you insure to it an immortality that is as substantial and inviolable as the universe itself; a conscious immortality, too, for the activity, in which the life of the individual persists, is ever conscious of its conditions and its consciousness is also the individual's consciousness.*

But here we come again to the sphere of religion, when our direct concern is not with what our view of the individual may mean to a philosophy of religion, but with what it means to a philosophy of history. To philosophy, however, the two are really inseparable. But for history, or for evolution, the organic function theory of individuality is of an immeasurable importance, since it makes

* I hardly need to call attention to the consistency of this view of the individual as in its very spatial and temporal character a transcending nature with the view of environment, suggested in the chapter on "Time," as the past and future contemporized with the present. The individual is a function, a relation, of environment.

history real. It offers the only conception of the individual, whether as nation or as man or as event or as any historical phenomenon, — the only conception, upon which a continuous, self-consistent history can be established. Institutions and historical phenomena of all sorts can be only the manifested definitions of existing tendencies, since they neither create nor destroy anything. Their definition has the effect merely of liberating for more controlled or more organic expression the tendencies which they define. And, in particular, the personal characters of history are but the definition, the focused individuation of general —but always perfectly real and concrete— activities in the social life. They are—in the familiar but somewhat misleading phrase already criticized here—applications, society's applications as well as their own, of the forces in the social life; and they make the social life, not conscious, but more clearly conscious of itself, and so stimulate a repetition or rather a more vital, a more responsible continuation of their careers in the life that gave them birth only to take them to itself again.

In chapters that are to follow, notably in the chapter: "The Great Man," examples of the historical process, here only generally recounted, will be given and discussed at some length, but in order at once to make the idea itself quite real, I will mention here perhaps the most striking example of all. In the simple fact, with the meaning suggested by the organic function theory, that Christ lives in Christendom today, the history of the past nineteen, twenty, centuries is made a real history, a history with which we now can directly identify ourselves. Perhaps in its doctrine of the after-life of Christ Christianity itself has had a better philosophy of history than it has been clearly aware of. Certainly—and our interest here is primarily historical, not religious, although we have a right to use the experiences of religion—the living Christ today is not some spirit, external to us that live, but is in and of the life and consciousness that we call ours.*

*See also my book "Citizenship and Salvation, or Greek and Jew," in which I have undertaken a study of the death of Socrates and the death of Christ from the standpoint defined here.

CHAPTER V.

PROGRESS.

NOW that we have considered in greater or in less detail, as the circumstances seemed to require, the character of time and causation and nature and individuality as data of history we should be able to free ourselves from the limitation of our vivisection and find in them all a living whole. We should see the history which they make as something that stands and moves before us. As a living or moving whole, however, they are what commonly we call progress. In progress, then, is the all-including and all-fulfilling datum of history to which we have at last to turn our attention.

In our conception of progress there are four principles that are all but axiomatic and that are four only until stated, when they become one. The first of these principles is this: Progress must always be of that which progresses. In other words, to be real or significant it can be only the expression of an already immanent and already active nature in that to which it is ascribed. Neither creation nor acquisition, neither destruction nor loss can enter into it. It forbids both outgrowth in the sense of complete elimination and genesis in the sense of sudden and wholly novel attainment. For a real and significant progress whatever comes to be is only the responsible, the consistent, the organically related expression of what both is and was. Nothing can be hereafter that already is not. Nothing is now that was not. Division of labor, to give a single example, is progress, because it neither adds to that in which it occurs nor substracts from it, but only expresses and fulfills it. True, progress has sometimes been predicated of a life that did not belong to and that accordingly was not responsible to that which lived, but only with the effect of turning the predicate into a mere empty name. A progress that is external, irresponsible, arbitrary, is worthless. It is not real. Where were the worth to a child in jumping a brook, if the act were not his?

But, secondly, progress can belong only to that which is conscious. Without consciousness the responsibility to self, which is necessary to the real and significant progress of anything, is not possible. Consciousness is the medium in which the past and the future of an activity are contemporized with the present and in being this it is what a physical science would call a principle of conservation. Conservation, however, means responsibility in any process that is subject to it. Hence evolution today for the sake of its own inner consistency as well as for the interpretation of its observations and discoveries has realized the supreme importance both of identifying life and consciousness, or rather of finding each of these intrinsic to the other, and of regarding the two as not local and temporary endowments but essential characters or functions in an indivisible universe. With consciousness an endowment the recognized conditions of expression are external to the conscious creature, and this is a fatal separation, but with consciousness the property of an organic universe such a fatal separation is impossible and a responsible fully conserved expression of self, which is a genuine progress, is assured.

And, thirdly, progress depends on individuals; on all individuals, however, not on anyone and not on a few; for individuality is nothing more nor less than a condition of consciousness. Only through individuals, perhaps the organs of your or my body, perhaps the separate members or the different classes of society, perhaps even all the manifold manifestations of life, can activity become conscious of itself and of the conditions of its expression. What above was called the focusing of individuals has as its great office the development of a clearer consciousness of self in the activity in which the individual appears. Or, again, the tension of organic relationship, which is consciousness, is also the sole foundation—but a very substantial foundation withal since the organic and the real are one—of individuality. Not to touch upon more complicated cases in this place, the three individual classes of human society, which contemporize, the first, the past and, the second, the future with the present and at the same time, in the third, do the peculiar and immediate tasks—shall we say the drudgery?—of the present, I mean in brief the leisured conventionalists, the advanced thinkers, and the workers or laborers in society, show—for the social consciousness—what the relation between consciousness and individuality is, and also how necessary both are to a genuine progress. Perhaps, too, some reader will comprehend me here with sufficient clearness to find another illustration in the three great realms of the inorganic so-called, the rational or human, and the animate or organic. But, if this second illustration fail, a third and last one is in the relation that every one of us conscious individuals bears to the life as a whole in which we find ourselves. Each of us—and it matters not into which social class we may be put, since from one or another point of view each one belongs to all the classes—is making society conscious of some detail of its natural responsibility.

Lastly, progress is neither of individual parts or organs, whether away from each other or away from the whole to which they belong, nor of the whole in the sense of a unity that is external to its parts, but of the whole and the parts as inseparable, of the whole in the expressed relations of the parts, and of the parts in their responsibility to each other or to the unity upon which their individuality depends. This is to say, what I think no one after reflection would deny, that coexisting parts or individuals, whether nations or social classes or persons or particular things or events of any kind, can never be either ahead of their times or behind their times. All that are at any time are present, and present not merely in the formal condition of time—time never is a merely formal condition —but also in their nature or character. The evolution of man, for example, has not been a growth out of or away from the primary conditions of his existence or "origin." His environment has evolved with him. And social classes, even if opposed, are neither ahead of nor behind each other, their conflict alone being evidence of their contemporaneity. To evolution and conspicuously to history in the narrower sense of human civilization the material contemporaneity of coexisting individuals is a principle whose importance could hardly be overstated. In the light of it consider the relation, not only of man to nature, but also of a great genius to his times, of rulers to those that are ruled, of the lawless to the law-abiding, of men to women, of capital to labor, and so on without limit.

But now, apart from these four principles or axioms that underlie a genuine progress and that, put in a single sum, make progress possible only to the activity of an organism—or to be very tautological—to the conscious activity of a system of different but mutually serving individuals, we may profitably undertake here a somewhat careful analysis of organic activity itself, with the hope of finding still more adequately aud still more positively in just what progress consists. Indeed, so far we have considered chiefly the conditions or limitations of a genuine progress, and now we have to see its possibilities. So far, at least to some, we may even seem to have turned progress into a sheer being what is and staying *in statu quo*, whereas we need to make sure that no such misinterpretation is the final interpretation.*

So, to begin the analysis at once, it is rationally necessary as well as empirically true, that activity, that any activity of individual, of society, or of the universe itself, be not the assumption of new relationships, nor escape from old relationships, but the expression and only the expression of existing relationships. The child that jumps the brook only expresses

---

*In the analysis that follows my community of thought with Prof. John Dewey, of the University of Chicago, will be evident to any one who has read the third chapter, "A General Study of Conduct," in his *Study of Ethics* (Ann Arbor, 1894.)

existing relationships; and, in general, were activity not so conditioned the criticism of causation or change in a former chapter would be meaningless, and we should be, in so far as we have accepted its conclusions, the victims of a fatal deception. As causation must be responsible, not arbitrary, so activity must be only expressive of what is. And, furthermore, the expression of activity always brings a clearer consciousness of its conditions or relations. Activity both has and brings—in the sense of more fully defines—a consciousness of its conditions, for the tension of the relationship expressed, which is consciousness, is essential to activity. This truth is very commonly recognized in popular thought. Action as being a process of self-discovery, as inducing its own interpretation, is a very commonplace idea, the burden of many sermons and an oft-recurring argument in political speeches, and the only variation that we are here making upon the popular notion is in our emphatic contention that the induced consciousness is intrinsic to the activity, being as much a condition as a result of it. Action does not induce consciousness in the sense of producing or obtaining something altogether new; it only clears or defines the consciousness that has already made the action possible. And this, it is plain, is only another way of repeating that consciousness is not a local and temporal endowment but a force or function that mediates among *all* the incidents of activity.*

With a clearer consciousness of its conditions activity is thrown into a conflict with itself. So to speak, the natural tension of its expression is made keener or sharper. The tendency to continue along the old paths conflicts with the recognized need of meeting the responsibility of the new experience; and this conflict is an unavoidable one because the recognized need is no mere future demand, the leap into the future having been taken already by the act itself. So to say, the activity *that has already taken place* is the future, for it is the source and object of the responsibility. Evidently, too, the conflict that arises in such a way can have no solution except such as will secure for the outgrown activity—for we can now call it that also—a more definite place in the system of possible acts that make up the agent's repertory, and that when brought to an

---

* Compare the principle of relativity in the modern theories of sensation. See also the discussion of the social consciousness in chapter vii.

organic unity will fully satisfy both the conservative tendency from the past and the demand of the new experience. Elimination of the outgrown activity would only intensify instead of solving the conflict. It would be no more adequate than a literal repetition. Two nations go to war and the conflict is plainly one of an already existing social life with itself, and in the outcome both of the contestants change their ways of life, but without necessarily losing their individuality. Indeed, they gain in individuality through the more responsible expression of it, that is to say, through the more social, the more organic expression of it, that the war induces, and when the war is over the social relation whose expression had made the war necessary is only freer to express itself than before. In like manner, an individual person finds himself opposed by his environment, but again the conflict is of an already expressed activity with itself. Indeed this illustration suggests what is becoming a familiar idea in current thinking. Any conflict is describable is one of two ways indifferently. It is either of an agent with himself or of the environment with itself. It is, very positively, not of one with the other in the meaning of the two as unrelated or only newly related factors. If we see the conflict as of an agent with himself, we recognize in it a thought process; if as of the environment with itself, a physical process; and on the one hand we have deliberation before volition, on the other latent preparation before kinetic manifestation, but the process is the same in both cases. The agent, although separated, is after all always a part of his own environment; and the environment, although separated, also shares in the relations that are already expressed in the action that brings on the conflict.

And, further, the consciousness that necessarily accompanies a conflict of this sort, that is both a condition and a result of the inducing activity, can have no goal but the organization of its elements or incidents, these being identical with the conditions of the activity itself. Indeed it is to be kept in mind that the "elements" of consciousness, whether viewed as subjective states or objective qualities, are only the relations or conditions of an already expressed activity. In general, then, consciousness as thus intimately involved in an activity that has originally related its subject and its object would only realize the law of the activity itself, and it would do this solely that in the law it may have a safe, because a fully satisfying motive to the expression of itself. Now a law, sometimes called a concept, is a principle of spatial and temporal determination of the different but related incidents of a process and in exactly this sense it is the natural object or content of consciousness. Only, neither object nor content is a safe term for use here. The meaning is not by any means that law as some abstract immaterial idea—in the understanding of a psychology that would separate thought and sensation or mind and body—is the object or the content of consciousness, but simply and inevitably that consciousness in and of itself is lawful, very much as nature is said to be lawful, the law and the process being one and the same thing. So, in summary, activity which induces a clearer consciousness of its own natural conditions and thereby sharpens the tension of its expression, its conflict with itself, is bound to develop as one of its direct incidents an ever more definitely lawful consciousness; or, to look to the other side of the same movement, the conditions of activity, which comprise what we find can be called the object of consciousness not without danger of serious misunderstanding, develop into a lawful environment; and with this development, whether of a lawful consciousness or of a lawful environment, the existing conflict approaches its solution in, not a new, but a freer expression of the original and ever-persisting activity. Moreover freer expression is just that in which progress consists.

Illustrations are not wanting. In chapters to follow this we shall find the evolution of human society, in short the history of civilization, to be true to the analysis of activity in general that has been given, but in this place I may appeal for illustration only to such activities as dealing an accurate blow, conducting a political campaign, building a house, or writing a book. In each of these the consciousness that accompanies the process—first—is always both a condition and a result of the process, and—second—is neither subjective nor objective because both subjective and objective or rather because only the tension of an existing organic relationship between subject and object, and—third—is the liberation of the process in its own realized lawfulness.

The liberation of activity, then, in its own

realized lawfulness is our formula for progress. But law, which is a term that can be applied indifferently to consciousness and to environment, to mind and to matter, just by dint of its serving to determine the organic relations of all of the details or incidents of activity or —and this is the same thing—of all of the possible activities in an agent's repertory, has a distinctly timeless character, being that in which—to recall a now familiar phrase—the future and the past are contemporized with the present. We may, therefore, in open recognition of this function of law reword our formula of progress as follows:

Progress is the timeless* because defining and contemporizing law of the past, whether as thought or as environment, becoming the motive, which is only the defined and contemporized future, of the present.

And progress is the all-including and all-fulfilling datum of history. Progress is history.

*Timeless, of course, in the sense that refers only to a fulfilment of the temporal, not to anything outside of the temporal.

Part II.
SOCIETY AND SOCIAL CHANGE.

CHAPTER VI.

THE GROUP IN GENERAL.

IT IS hardly necessary to say that society as well as individuality or any of the other things considered in the foregoing chapters is a datum of history, but also it is hardly necessary to say that thought progresses only by changing its standpoint and its machinery. In this second part of our present study it is as if we were too near to history itself, to its life and our identity with it to speak of mere data of history. Society and social change are history itself. With them we are ever identifying the progress that we have found history to be. Political science, the science of social life, and history are considered nowadays as one and the same thing.

But our idea of society must not be superficial. It must be consistent with our idea of the group in general, just as in considering individuality we felt obliged to think of atoms as well as of persons. Human society is a group of individuals and in the group as such there are certain characteristics that it is well to notice, so to speak, without any political prejudices.

So, to begin with, *any* group is a more or less definitely organized manifold of different individuals. This is to say that a group is a differentiated whole whose differences contribute to or are identical with its unity. A chair, for example, is a group of many things, but even such of the parts as the legs or the rounds that seem alike in themselves are all different as parts of the chair. A circle is a group of a number of arcs or of a number—of course an infinite number—of points that in themselves are all alike but in the circle different, the unity or integrity of the circle requiring their perfect differentiation. The tenth dollar in a sum of ten dollars is different from the ninth or the eighth, because ten dollars as a group will satisfy a different interest from that which nine or eight would satisfy. The family circle, the nations of the earth, the objects in a room, the heavenly bodies, are all groups of which the principle, stated above, that unity and differences are inseparable, is irrefutably true. Things in general, if seen as many are different and if seen as different are related as the members of some group. Not that the relation, the organization of the differences is always altogether definite, but simply that the fact itself of an organic differentiation is essential to any group.

Any group, then, is a group with parts or members that are the related means to some one end or with differences that co-operate in some one function or activity. On any other assumption the inseparableness of the unity and the differences would be meaningless, since only in the adaptation of means to end is unity made to be intrinsic to differences. But why posit an end as a function or activity? Because a group whose differences are also its unity must always be more than a formal composition, and because only its implication in an activity can make it more. In itself it must be essentially dynamic. What holds a chair together but gravity? Gravity, then, is the process to which the chair is a means. True, somebody of a very practical turn may say that the chair is held together because it is something to sit in, but sitting is only one of many other adaptations on the part of living creatures to the force of gravity. So, in general, the end to which any group is a means is a positive activity which the group's differential unity both belongs to and shares in. I say "shares in," for I think no one would deny of the chair—to return to that—that its parts exercise the force of gravity as well as adjust themselves to it.

But a group to which activity is essential, a group that in itself is dynamic, being the immanently active expression of unity in differences or of differences in unity, is an organism. Is this to say that *any* group lives? It certainly is, *but not on the endowment plan*. It is to recognize in every group a tension. The tension is between the group's own local and momentary existence and the larger activity in which the group shares and to which the group is a means. Thus, the chair lives through the fact of its being in a tension with gravity as a universe force. Gravity both holds it together and in course of time destroys or disintegrates it. The chair, or any other group, in this way may be said to live its own death. It lives its own death, just because it is a group and as a group is responsible intensively to itself and extensively* to the force to which it owes its existence. Our

---

*Except that the extensive is always only the more intensive.

friend of the practical turn would no doubt express the same idea by saying that chairs have come and gone, new and different and perhaps better chairs arising to take their place, for the simple reason that the activity of sitting, which brought them into life, for the sake of its own more adequate expression has required also that they should pass away. Gravity, however, to which sitting is an adaptation, is not life—is it? Perhaps not, although gravity has something to do with the conservation of an organic universe. Sitting is not life either, but it is quite in order to suggest that living creatures sometimes sit and, as indicated before, in doing so are not merely adapting themselves to gravity but also identifying themselves with it. Too often we forget—do we not?—that adaptation is always identification, that the conditions of any activity always share positively in the activity. Should we remember this at all times, some unnaturally difficult problems would turn as unnaturally simple.

And in any case the group as a group—and this means *any* group—is an organism, active and alive and responsible, but—to repeat—*not on the endowment plan.*

CHAPTER VII.

THE HUMAN GROUP OR SOCIETY.

THE human group or society is also an organism, active and alive and responsible but not on the endowment plan.

From a chair to society! This is a jump indeed, and I know too well that there are many who will promptly refuse to take it even with the help of such a profound insight into the nature of *any* group as was reached in the previous chapter! Still I do not despair of getting even the most cautious of jumpers across the awful chasm, although to get them over I shall probably have to do more than suggest to them that chairs as well as gravity have played their part and are still playing their part in the life and consciousness of a *sometimes* sedentary human society. This suggestion, however, should not be dismissed as altogether impertinent.

Of course at the present time the organic character of society is a much discussed question, and as is usual in such cases the discussion implies an ignorance, an incomplete knowledge, of the things discussed. To understand anything is to have to limit it to nothing, to find in it a universe-truth. To say that society is not an organism and that some individual mass is an organism is not yet to know just what an organism really is. But you remind me that most if not all thinkers today admit the organic character of society. They do not, however, admit it unqualifiedly, and their qualifications show that the term is so imperfectly understood that it is in their thinking at war with itself, meaning two things instead of only one. Society, they say, is an organism, but not as the individual is an organism. It is an organism only ideally, or only spiritually, or only psychologically, or only physically, and so on, with some rhyme possibly but not much reason. The term "only," like fire, is very useful when controlled but very dangerous to play with.

Herbert Spencer is a case in hand. He is willing to apply to society the name organism, but not without qualification, not to the detriment of his individualism; and in consequence his individuals lose their own organic character.

Let us see how this is. He draws analogies between the organism—the living individual of biology—and society, but also he discovers points of difference that qualify the organic character of society almost out of existence. Thus, society and the organism are alike in that their growth brings increase in mass, increase in complexity of structure, and increase in the interdependence of parts, and in that the whole has permanence although the parts die, but different in that society as society, unlike the organism, has no distinct form, no continuous tissue and no local consciousness, all its parts or members being conscious, and in that the parts of society, unlike those of the organism, are free to move autonomously. But here is a lot of falsehoods or at least a lot of statements that are flagrantly superficial. The organism, even the individual organism, is not what Spencer says it is in so many words. Mass as mass has nothing to do with organic character, nor has mere complexity, and the whole that is really permanent is not something that can even for a moment be separated from its parts, and if the real organism, the individual organism, has such a distinct form, why is biology still busy over her microscopes? Can the naked eye be trusted in the case of society when it is not trusted in that of the individual? And who has ever seen real continuity? Visible continuity in itself does not make or unmake an organism, since the only final test of continuity is in expressed relationship. In Spencer's sense even protoplasm is not continuous. Furthermore, in regard to the matter of consciousness, the individual organism as well as society is conscious in all of its members. In other words sensation, or consciousness generally, is a function of the individual as a whole, not the special action or condition of certain separate organs. And, to conclude this arraignment of Spencer's idea of the organism, the parts of the individual have in reality as much autonomy as the members of society. A difference in degree there may be between the freedom in the one case and the freedom in the other, but such difference instead of denying the principle that is involved only asserts it. Only when the members of society are free autonomously to move through each other or through walls and to lift themselves by their boot-straps and do other things in violation of the organizing unity of their universe, only then can I find their freedom, their individualism, different in kind from that of the parts of my own body or of any other living mass.

But Spencer can be met also on his own ground. His standpoint is a physical one, and physical science, looking at the life of society, at the body in which that life is expressed, has no trouble at all in finding massiveness, continuity, localization, and restraint or confinement of individuals, which Spencer would make the criteria of organic character, in society. Society, then, as Spencer himself uses the term, is as organic as anything else. Spencer seems to me like a man who has pushed his fingers up through a hole in a sheet of paper and looking at them argues to individualism from their apparent isolation and autonomous wriggling. But you object to such a comparison? The fingers, you grant, are not really detached, but the members of society are. Detached, perhaps; but in any case not unrelated. Stones, too, are detached, but for the sake of an organizing natural law, not in spite of it.

Spencer's case is altogether a typical one. Spencer, like many others, although he passes as an evolutionist, is not enough of an evolutionist to identify human life with the nature from which it is supposed to have sprung. He makes the nature of man something by itself. Like the other forms of life, with which he deals, man is not seen as in himself already adapted to the presented conditions of human activity. Witness the negative, the irrational element in environment, which Spencer calls the Unknowable and which can not but have the effect of separating man from himself or—as the same thing—from the conditions of his life. But to divide man, to make the living man and the material man, or the spiritual man, two separate creatures instead of one creature is at once to put the organism, whether individual or social, wholly out of the question. An organism lives the life of its environment. With conditions external in their nature it can have nothing to do; or, if it does relate itself to them, it can be seen only as Spencer sees it, namely, in terms of massiveness, continuity, localization, restraint of its members, and so on, and this is to say that it is not really seen at all. And, as with Spencer's, so with anybody's division of human nature. It puts a real organic character, whether of individual or of society, wholly out of the question. The concept of the organism, like that of evolution to which it belongs, depends on the unity of all the phases of life, of the physical and the animate and the rational and the spiritual, and sociologists or political scientists of any kind, who would deny organic character to society or who would in any of the many ways qualify their admission of the term organism would do well, of course in the first place to discover if they really know what an individual organism as an organism is, but especially in the second place to determine what their particular division of human nature is and how far they are seriously willing to make it. If human nature is indivisible, if there is only one man in any of us, then as individuals or as society or as either in the other we are living the life of the conditions of our life and this is but to say that we are living a strictly organic life. Fully to realize this organic life we must expect to have to go deeper, to look deeper, than human natu.e, for just the reason suggested. Human nature is more than, it is always deeper than itself. The universe is in it. And for us, who are in search of a real principle and accordingly can not stop with anything short of a real principle, no depths can be too deep.

Society, then, as a group of human beings whose nature is one nature and is one with all nature, is like any group; it is an organism. Wherever the members of *any* group are obliged to adjust themselves to each other and to their environment in the interests of an all-controlling, all-including law or process, be the law or the process physical—as in the case of gravity—or psychical or spiritual or of any other character you like, they comprise in their nature and activity what is essentially an organism.

And an organic society, furthermore, has both a social consciousness and a social will.

Evidences of a social consciousness are in the fact of a common environment; in the fact, if not of a common language, at least of different languages that are translatable more or less easily; in the fact of such social institutions as the state, the church, the school, and the factory; and in the fact of all the different means of intercourse, the instruments of communication and of transportation and the like. These evidences, moreover, are all reducible to one, to the simple fact of the community of nature in all men and the community of man with all nature. Psychologist and political scientist at the present time are coming to look upon environment, the object or the content of consciousness, as the central, the organizing unity of all the different means to a social life. They see it as the social institution of all social institutions, as the whole of which language and the other things that were mentioned are but special differentiated expressions or relations.

But one's view of the nature of the social consciousness will depend very naturally on what one supposes the relation to environment to be. To speak strictly, the unity of all the different means to a social life in environment is not a possible idea without a clear appreciation of the unity of human nature and of man with all nature, but we may neglect this necessity of thought and consider, as if they were equally possible, the two cases of those, first, who would separate man from some or all of the conditions of his life—or aspects of his environment—and, second, who would recognize positively and directly the unity of man and the sphere in which he lives. In the first case, the case of the separation, as has been pointed out already, neither society as society nor its members as individuals can be supposed to have a genuinely organic character; and, as to consciousness, this, in the individuals is a mere endowment or God-sent—when not devil-sent—gift and in society an equally although more obviously arbitrary or irrational and so unreal possession. The individual is conscious, but the consciousness is not his; and the consciousness of society is external to the humanity of society, being "given," infallible, and referred to a language and a system of other institutions that are as dead to those who use them, as brutally fixed and as intellectually empty, as the external environment in general to which they belong, and that serve therefore either to reduce the members of society to a lifeless level or—which in effect is the same thing—to create inviolable differences among them or among the classes into which they may be divided.

Subjectively consciousness as an endowment is always localized or enthroned in some particular member or members, and at first thought it seems strange that those who have separated man from the sphere of his life and have given certain of man's parts an arbitrary right to his consciousness should have denied a local habitation and sometimes even a name to the social consciousness. What does an absolute monarchy or an infallible papacy or an arbitrary individual leadership of any kind mean but a social consciousness that is at once an endowment and a localized function? Is a ruling individual—or possibly a ruling class—any less real or any less local or any less arbitrary in the thought or consciousness that it exercises than the brain or than a group of special sense-organs? Given a monarchical or a feudalistic psychology, and you get also a monarchial or a feudalistic politics; and yet the advocates of the former find the social consciousness in the latter a mere abstraction. This, I have said, seems strange, but after all the case is the same as that of Spencer's organism, which was denied to society but affirmed of the individual, and just because it was not a genuine organism at all. Consciousness on the localized endowment plan is not consciousness but unconsciousness or mere physical quality. It appears to be one of the offices of the life and nature of society to reveal to the individual his erroneous views of himself. Above Spencer's inorganic society exposed his individual organism, and here an unconscious society has exposed a conscious, a selfishly conscious individual.

So, almost in spite of ourselves, we are brought to our second case, the case of those who would recognize positively and directly the unity of man and the sphere in which he lives. For these both individual and society are organic and consciousness, at once individual and social, is in and of the life itself that the organism expresses, being as truly a condition as a consequence of it, and is referred to a language and to other institutions that are themselves vital incidents of it and grow consistently with it, serving neither to level nor to separate individuals or classes, but to unite them by sanctioning and mediating their peculiar differences. Environment, the unity of all the means to a social life and thought, is looked upon and is to be resorted to as the great mediator of differences, and language, as only a very highly developed relation to environment, can no longer serve, or be imagined to serve, as a medium of universally valid truths, a repository of dogmas, but only, so to speak, as a *tertium quid* in which individuals can agree to differ. The days are past when men can think in chorus. They have gone with the days of the immutable species and irresponsible individual.

Not for a moment can anybody conclude from what has been said that there are two consciousnesses, an individual consciousness and a social consciousness. The conscious individual is in himself socially conscious and the conscious society is in itself a society of conscious individuals.

But, objects somebody, this is all very well; only it fails to account for that undoubtable "public opinion," which belongs to nobody, and yet the searching eye of which is felt by everybody. "Public opinion" has standards, I am reminded, that are at least relatively fixed and arbitrary or irrational. Well, I can only say in reply to this, what I think is incontrovertible, that the objector, in so far as he finds "public opinion" fixed and irrational, is identifying it with phrases or customs or institutions. These, however, do not represent the real public opinion; they are dying creatures when not mature wholly unsubstantial ghosts. In just so far as opinion becomes public and fixed, it loses its authority in consciousness. The mere machinery of the social life is not its consciousness. Sometimes it may seem to be, but every one knows that it is not. At a "function," what but "public opinion" and its commonplaces ever finds expression, but how truly every one is thinking of what he does not hear and of what he does not say! No wonder that those who would identify the social consciousness with society's conventionalities can see it only as vague or abstract, as purely spiritual in the sense of external and unreal.

But the true nature of the social consciousness will be still more clearly understood by us when we have seen in just what the social will consists. Political scientists have fallen into the habit of saying that the state must not be identified with the government, and this seems to me to be only their way, or one of their ways, of saying, what has been said above, that the social consciousness must not be identified with the mere machinery of the social life, and what is now to be said, that the social will must not be identified merely with the visible law or authority. If the will and the visible authority are identified, then the will becomes the interest or motive of an abstractly universal nature rather than the interest or motive of either society as society or any of its particular members. Such a will is a purely common will or—by a strange but thoroughly logical connection between the opposites—the separate wills of wholly unrelated individuals. It need hardly be said that the divisibility of the social will and the much discussed divisibility of sovereignty are one and the same problem.

Make the social will a strictly common will and you get in return only the most extreme individualism in the social life, for the common will that is responsible to no interests of its own is bound to relate itself to the interests of anybody and everybody. Thomas Hobbes and even Rousseau—or perhaps Rousseau more clearly than anybody else—found a common social will and absolute individualism the two sides of one and the same truth.

The social will, however, if social because common, can be nobody's will; and, if will simply that it may be somebody's, can not be social. To separate the will of society either in the way of an absolute monarchy or in the way of a purely individualistic democracy, is to lose sight of the true nature of will itself or of the true nature of both society and its members. Will is not a something that controls life from without, just as society and individuality, as the two recognized sources of control, are not external to each other. Will and life, whether the life of the individual or the life of society, are one and the same thing. The natural, immanent, self-determined compulsion of what is already active at any time and place is the only will, the only social will, that we can be serious about. Is the will of society, forsooth, different from that of a mother with her child, or of a runner in a race, or of a machinist at his work? Voluntary acts, individual and social, are only justifications of actual conditions, the fulfilments of existing activities, or suppose we say almost technically the reactions of adapted structures on their *sympathetic* environments. Society, then, being an organism, and the social consciousness being social only because individual and individual only because social, the social will can have no reality except as the expression of the existing social life, the maintenance of the organic unity of individual interests or relations. The truly social will is of such a nature that it is a necessity inherent in the individual will. It is, in short, the tension of a social individuality.

A single conclusion from this account of the will of society will serve to illustrate it. Thus, if the will of society is what we say it is, then we should be able to show definitely that the act of any individual not only is the act of society but also is recognized by society as its own. This, however, in both of its counts, can be shown very easily; and I take the most unfavorable case available. What criminal ever does his own crime alone? Nay, who are his accomplices but those who, although living in the law, have induced his act by helping to make it possible? The social life in which a crime is possible is not determined by the criminal any more than it is determined by his accusers. His act, then, is their act; his commission, their omission. The mere machinery of the social life is that in which crime and lawfulness act hand in hand. And society knows this; society constantly recognizes it. Just as no parent punishes his child without feeling that he should himself receive the punishment, or rather without actually receiving it in some way, direct or indirect, so society takes her revenge on the transgressor only to suffer herself and to realize that his act was as much hers as his. Human history is but a startling record of the awakened self-convicting consciousness of those who have condemned their fellows, and their awakening, moreover, has somehow always been as much the cause as the consequence of the condemnation. Not that any offense is to be supposed any less offensive or any offender any less responsible in the light of this history, but from the fact that society shares in the offenses of her members no offense is either wholly unpardonable or wholly invaluable. In the phrases of religion the conviction of sin is both forgiving and saving. In their crimes, then, as well as in their lawful deeds, the members of society are servants both of their own lives and of the social life to which they belong. As was indeed said here many pages back, individuality has its only reality in a process by which life becomes conscious *of its own conditions.*

So, in summary of this chapter, the human group or society is an organism; it is conscious in its individuals; and it has a will that is not common, that is not divided, but is the compulsion inherent in the single activity of its individual members.

CHAPTER VIII.

THE DOUBLE RESPONSIBILITY OF SOCIETY.

LIKE the chair or like any group society lives its own death; for society, any society, has a responsibility that is at once intensive and extensive, at once to its own manifest life and to nature* as a whole, and sooner or later under the tension of this double responsibility it can not but outgrow itself.

In positive history, to which we are now ready to turn with a directness that has not been possible before or rather that has not been as apparent as it can now become, any particular society is particular by virtue of a domain, a consciousness of a past, and a distinct activity. Only in proportion as it has these is it separated from nature. Its peculiarity, it is true, or the separation is often explained by reference to geographical condi-

---

* I say nature here and in other places, because the term is so inclusive. Nature includes not only other societies but also other manifestations of life in general, and it includes besides the deeper and undiscovered or only partially discovered life of the society itself that finds it external.

tions or to other physical conditions and sometimes by reference to a divine guidance, but in the special meanings usually intended neither of these references can be allowed here. The determination can not come from without, whether from a designing God or from an external nature. Peculiar environing conditions can not of themselves be said to make peculiar societies when human nature is in itself as broad and as deep as the whole to which it belongs, when man and nature or nature and man are one. Moreover—and this comes near to being only the converse of what has just been said—for a society to have become peculiar or individual, for it to have become separated from nature, is for it also to have transcended itself, to have come into a conflict that is indifferently describable as with nature or with itself. Has it a certain territory? The boundaries were drawn only to define a developed and recognized relation to the life beyond them. Has it a treasured past? It has begun to realize that it sprang from a life that was before it was? Or has it a special and consciously conducted pursuit such as agriculture, or herding, or commerce, or anything else you like? The pursuit has an already appreciated, an already determining relation to the other activities of nature's life. Thus, in any one of the three ways, in which we can see the isolation of a society, the limit is set only as it is transcended. Consider how merely in becoming Greek the Greek people entered into an ever strengthening, not a weakening relation to the Barbarians; and, similarly, the Jewish people to the Gentiles; and we American people to the peoples east and west, north and south of our national borders.

A peculiar society, then, is not really an isolated society, and in expressing itself it is bound to maintain both sides of its responsibility. It can not escape the conflict with its own individuality. To the casual observer expression of self might be expected only to intensify an original isolation, but casual observation is not to be trusted, for expression even while intensifying not an original isolation but an original individuality is also affirming ever more directly, ever more positively the relation between the individual and what is without. This is almost paradoxical, and yet what thoughtful historian has ever failed to recognize that throughout the course of history the conquerors and the conquered in any struggle have shared with each other both their victory and their defeat? But let us see for ourselves.

There can be no doubt that whenever a society awakens to a sense of its own importance and so to a sense of its opposition to the life without it enters upon a more intense expression of itself, and this would seem to lead to a growing separation instead of to a growing identification of the inner and the outer, but a result must always be true to its origin and in the case in hand the origin is as internal to the society involved as it is external. The awakening and the opposition are due as much to a motive at home as to a stimulus abroad. The story, I say, is the same as that of the chair, which gravity holds together and which gravity destroys. The people themselves have done something to make the conflict, not the conflict comes as if out of a clear sky; and the more intense the ensuing self-expression becomes the more truly does the society come into a recognized conflict with itself and so even invite attack from without. Indeed, in ways that are startling when first observed, a society that intensifies its own individuality, that would even isolate itself, does but co-operate with its opponents in bringing about some kind of a revolution in its own life, and the strange co-operation although for a time held from view is not by any means unseen from the beginning and in the end it comes to be more or less directly and openly avowed. Intensification of individuality implies—does it not?—the mere cultivation of one's peculiar life, a living in one's own way simply for the sake of living in one's own way, and upon this plan, upon the plan that turns life into a cult, formalism and disintegration are sure to ensue.

But, again, a people finds itself confronted with a great war, a great danger. So great is the danger that an invasion may be threatened. And who brought on the war? So far as I know, no honest historian has ever exonerated either of the parties to a war. A war springs out of the expression of some vital relation between the contestants, out of a community of nature, out of some common interest. An approaching enemy, moreover, even when barbarian or wholly uncivilized, is sure to bring the reproach of a forgotten past, the call to a neglected duty; is sure to arouse a dormant conscience. Should the hosts of China come against us today, just this would be true of their coming; and just this was very true when Xerxes and the others moved upon Greece. And how does a war affect a people? It affects them exactly as any activity that they feel responsible for has to affect them. It affects them exactly as reproval, sense of neglect, and aroused conscience are always effective. They get bravery? Yes, and also bravado. Strength? And conceit. Unity? And discord. Patriotism? And treachery. Was ever a war that did not bring both the one and the other of these things?

War, then, which is as much a conflict with self as with an enemy without, which rises as individuality arises, and is indeed only individuality's conflict with itself, exhibits to us a process by which a society may be said to be put beside itself, or to be alienated from itself. From its very inception war casts discredit on the life of the people by making them, as never before, conscious of what they are doing. The life, although discredited, may long continue, but ever more and more for appearance's sake only. The common cause that the war makes is weakening to all the personal and sectional differences upon which the society has always depended, and it serves accordingly to make the people external to their own activity, or, as said above, to alienate the society from itself. The more definite consciousness of what they have been doing comes with a decrease in the sense of responsibility to it. In short, from its very inception, a war brings with it into the life of the people an ever strengthening undercurrent of what is, sooner or later, recognized as cosmopolitanism, or world-wide interest, and in the end an entire civilization may be swept away thereby. And if a world-wide interest is what induces the war, what other outcome should be expected than just this of a more clearly defined world-wide interest. War, like conflict in general, is only the definition of activity.

Hereafter we shall have to follow the process of society's alienation from itself, in considerable detail, but for the present the process itself, as we have it, suggests to us a way of reducing the activity of a society, in which it meets its double responsibility, to certain stages. First, there is the stage of society's at-one-ness with self; second, of its complete alienation from self; and, third, of its restoration to self. Of course, of the third stage we have not yet seen anything except by implication, but its general nature is evident enough. In positive history the three are marks of the orient that was, the occident that is, and the reunion of the two that not yet is; or, within narrower limits, of the Greek life that was, the Roman life that was and still is, and the Christian—or European-American—that is or is coming to be; or, still more narrowly, of the colonial life in our own history, the period of sectionalism—have we passed it yet?—and the future to which we look and which even now we think we see.

These stages, then, are our next concern. To begin with, we shall define them somewhat fully, each for itself, and in its relation to the others; and then having, as it were, determined our landmarks, we shall give special attention to the transitions, to the alienation as a process that is teeming with important details and to the restoration that is not less important to us and that is indeed the process in which we are likely to see the life of our own time.

But before we turn to these new interests there is something that should be said, by way of caution, of this reduction of a process to its stages. Thus, in the first place, a series of stages must always be somewhat schematic. The three stages of a society's activity are all of them, even the second one, extremes. Extremes, however, are never found in real life, and when we think of them they are significant only for the principle which they embody, only for the activity which they abstractly define. Sometimes we describe a curve by its stages. Thus, we say it begins here; it reaches a maximum or minimum here; and it ends here; and these stages appear to us different even in kind; but they are only the terms of a relationship expressed in what is a perfectly uniform process. As with a described curve, then, so with a recounted history. The past as a first stage is but—and here is a reminiscence—a contemporary of the present, and the future as a last stage is also but a contemporary of the present, while the present itself as the intermediate stage is the activity in which the relationship of the other two is in expression. Furthermore there is a sense, not unfamiliar to us, and highly important to all who would avoid any misconceptions, in which the stages of any process are materially as well as formally coexistent. Indeed formal coexistence and formal sequence alike have been impossible to us. The sequent and the coexistent are one, action being but the expression in sequence of the persistent relations of the coexistent. Thus, *is* the orient as indicative of a life at one with itself—the first stage—or *was* it? Both. And *is* the reunion of occident and orient—the third stage—or *is it to be?* Both. And, finally, in the relation of the sequent to the coexistent we see once more the danger of too arbitrarily identifying the stages of a process with localities. To repeat from above what was but another way of expressing the thought here, peculiar environing conditions, in other words, peculiar localities can not of themselves be said to make peculiar societies when the human nature out of which societies are built is as broad and as deep as the whole to which it belongs. In space and in time alike whole and part, unity and difference, the undetermined and the local or momentary can not be separated. Coexistences are materially cotemporary and sequences are only the expression of the organic unity of coexistences.

Is this too metaphysical or too philosophical even for the philosophers themselves? Possibly, but I cannot doubt that such of them as will think as well as read will find a truth in it. The language is simple enough and it means exactly what it says. Science, it seems to me, after busying herself so long with stages or moments or degrees, needs to be aroused to a real responsibility to her own words. Stages in themselves are not history any more than positions are a curve or than places are a journey. History transcends its stages and its localities by persistently contemporizing and universalizing them.

CHAPTER IX.

THE STAGES OF SOCIETY'S ACTIVITY.

AS already given, the three stages of a society's activity are those of its at-one-ness with self, of its alienation from self, and of its restoration to self; and we found them significant, not in themselves, but only in their relationship or in the single activity that they define. For purposes of discussion, however, we have to keep them apart; and here, with the philosopher's license, we may even assign to each one of them its own peculiar formula; to the first: *what is, is*, which is the formula of life as naive; to the second: *what is not, is*, the formula of life as external to itself or subject to the unnatural or supernatural; and again to the third: *what is, is*, which, although verbally a repetition, is here the formula, not of the naive, but of the supernatural naturalized or of the natural as rationally free.

But the stages of a society's activity, the stages of social evolution, have something besides these interesting mottoes. They have incidents or conditions. Accordingly our task is now to discover exactly what the incidents are in each case. Of course, the incidents as they appear will illustrate the mottoes, but the mottoes need the incidents to make them real. So, entering upon our task, we are to ask of each one of the three stages the following questions: Who is the typical individual? Upon what is sovereignty based? What is the natural form of government? Of what character is law? What is the true form of property? What, of literature? And what, of religion? These are searching questions, and although they involve us in a discussion that may prove a little tedious on account of its verbal repetitions, or, let us say on account of the rattle of its machinery, the work itself—even with the noise—is well worth our while.

In the first stage, that of society's at-oneness with itself, the personal individual, the social type, is the naive or unreflective laborer. The term laborer, however, is almost too specific or too technical, but suffice it to say that no distinctions of class are intended. The basis of sovereignty is the social life itself; the life, this is to say, rather than the will, since a social will has not yet been aroused. The form of government is that of a direct monarchy, which is also a direct democracy, as illustrated in patriarchism, or perhaps in the early Greek communities whose kings (βασιλεῖς) were the direct agents of the people. Law is personal command. Property consists in land or nature in general, held in common, and in the products of nature, which are exchanged through barter, there being no selected medium of exchange. As to literature, properly speaking, there is none, although in ballads and stories or yarns of a traditional and often mythical character that pass from mouth to mouth the germs of a literature are present. And, lastly the religion is naturistic or—for this seems a better word—absolutely simple, being without question and without dogma. God is near to man; nay, He and man are one.

A golden age, you say? Yes, and significant exactly as that is significant. Of it, as well as of each of the two other stages, we must remember that it is an extreme, a limit, and so in a sense only a philosopher's fancy, and even to illustrate it as a whole or in any of its parts—as occasionally I have tried to—is to be almost untrue to it, to force it perhaps a little ahead of itself. But without illustration, you insist, it is empty, meaningless. So it is, until we can observe it from the standpoint of another stage.

In the second stage, then, the stage of the alienation, the typical individual is the soldier, again to use a technical term without intending any distinction of class. The soldier in general is he who lives beside himself, whose activity is not his own, who belongs to a society that is physically a mere mechanism of differences established from without and spiritually—the spiritual being that which is not, the external—a perfect community, a company of individuals all alike. Living beside himself, alienated from himself, he is ready at any moment to die, his very alienation being a sanction of any change, however violent, in his life. In a society of soldiers, further, the sovereignty rests on worldly might, which is purely physical force, or on spiritual authority. In history, when God has appointed the king, might has always been a basis of right; and naturally enough, because might is only external authority, as it were, in the flesh. Might is only the reality of the spiritual.* But, next, the government is an absolute monarchy, the

*Cf. pp. 63-64.

monarch—a soldier himself—being not a worldly individual, but the universal individual, and in this character even representative of his subjects,* since in a society where all are spiritually equal any one—when physically and spiritually equipped—can represent all. And the law is given, traditional, statutory; not the mandate of an individual, for that would make it worldly and so would deny the alienation, but, if I may borrow the term, scriptural, and not with any mixture of equity, for that too is worldly or responsible to differences. Property consists in mere domain and in money as some simple in the sense of directly derived or unchanged product of nature, both of these being abstract or universal, or suppose we say—appropriately enough—unworldly forms of property. Mere domain—unimproved nature—and coin are property freed of all the specific relations of life. Infinite possibilities of relation are in them, but for themselves alone they are the natural possessions of the unworldly individual, exacting no worldly duties, depending on no worldly ties, being valuable merely

* The fact, here plainly indicated, that even absolute monarchy, is a form of representative government is one indication among many of the ways in which these stages of society's growth are as contemporary as sequent.

in possession, and being freely, that is, without danger of loss or injury, inheritable. The soldier, obviously, must have a freely inheritable property. Payment in anything else he cannot but refuse. In history, now to give the dangerous illustration, when property has had the form of landed estates and coin, mere possession constituting right and might being the beginning and the end of possession, the property-owner has worked his land and earned his coin only through slaves or servants of some kind, being himself a military lord, not a ploughman and not even a "gentleman-farmer;" and in just this separation of master and laborers, of will and activity, we can see the social implications of property as here considered. With society alienated from itself both are will and activity necessarily apart and apart also are the agents and the return for what they do. But, to continue, to this second stage belong a given, ready-made literature and—in the technical sense—a revealed religion. Language has no life of its own, but it is the repository of truth as something absolute and unchanging; and perhaps in a single book or in a single man religion may have its beginning and its end. Original thinking is as unnatural as it is sacrilegious. Copying, engrossing, memorizing, and possibly logical gymnastic and textual annotation are as far as the intellectual class—the priesthood—can ever allow itself to go, but these things it will do with a faithfulness and a patience that only a soldier's implicit devotion can make possible. Is not language the Word, the Incarnate Word?

But, lastly, when as in the third stage society is restored to itself, the typical individual is the mechanic—again without intending any distinctions of class—in whom, as it were, the dead soldier has his resurrection. Thus the mechanic is the skilled laborer. Not only like the soldier has he a place in society, but also is he directly or consciously and voluntarily responsible to it. He is as much a leader as one led. He has identified himself with the freedom of the military life to which as only a mechanical part he had previously belonged. The activity in which he shared slavishly is become his activity. In short, he has brought his other self, his unworldly self, in which he had been so isolated, into the world, finding it real and as spiritual as real in the life that is. And with this finding on his part the society to which he belongs and the social life are no longer separated, but are restored to each other. The state and its members become one, and in the social will, as the will of a self-conscious organism, the sovereignty resides, and the government takes the form of a constitutional democracy, in which the constitution is adaptive or elastic, being regarded not as something to which society owes its existence, but as something which owes its existence to society, as something which is definitive only, not creative. Law, in the special sense, is also elastic, equity—conspicuously absent in the second stage—being here the moving spirit; and property is either machinery, which comprises all improved natural resources, all applications of natural force, or credit, which is that in which productive power or skill is made the sole right to property and so also the sole medium of exchange. So long as any single natural product or commodity, such as gold or silver or anything else, is the medium, or as unimproved nature is the form of property, just so long mere possession constitutes the right to property and ownership is also an arbitrary or military leadership of labor, the will or power of action as well as its return being separated from action itself; but for the freed individualism, the skilled labor, of this third stage, in which no man can be set beside himself, or alienated from himself, the arbitrary medium, whether of the silver-heresy, or the gold-dogma or the paper-lunacy, is impossible. Credit, then, be it said again, as the subjective or personal, and machinery as the objective or natural form of property, credit being the recognized capacity of production and machinery the material means to the production, are here the only possible forms of property. In them capitalist and laborer become one. That property, however, so conditioned depends on a well-defined social consciousness, on a freedom of prompt and accurate information the world over, and on an untrammeled movement and interaction among individuals, on a freedom of safe and rapid transportation to any point, is self-evident. In olden times all roads led to Rome, and the day came when over the roads hurried, not Rome's couriers and not Rome's armies, but barbarians, who dealt a fatal blow to militarism; and today we see how roads and wires are breaking the strength of the military industrialism that our unskilled labor and our irresponsible capital* have helped each other to maintain so long. But, finally, in the third stage literature is mediative, language being no dead and formal thing, but alive and responsive, and the thought expressed in it being no abstract truth, fixed and as meaningless as fixed, but a moving, liberating idea that is one with life itself; and religion is a natural religion, in which God is immanent in what his creatures do, their acts having a positive share in his creation, and in which the truth that faithfully and responsibly defines the condition of life to those that live is the only real, because the only effective or answerable prayer. Worship is skill in the social life, not ritual; and the church is society itself, not a mass of bricks and stained glass.

Utopian vision? Yes, but also an actual condition, a present already active impulse as well as a future dream; a life, in which the present is now transcending its own limitations; and so worthy of our attention.

And here I will repeat the illustrations, that were suggested before, of the three stages of society's growth: the orient, the occident, and

---

* By irresponsible capital I mean capital to which possession is the only basis of right.

the now rising restoration of each to the other; Greek life, Roman life, and the moving Christianity of Europe and America today; and colonial America, sectional America—covering the period from the Revolution through to the Rebellion, perhaps to the present time—and America as a truly organized democracy. But, as has been said in so many words, such illustrations are likely to be as obscure as luminous. Still we may use them if we use them cautiously, ever remembering that the sequent and the coexistent are fundamentally one. The past is always present in another locality, and coexistences, in spite of their local differences, are materially as well as formally contemporary. History ever transcends both its stages and its localities by persistently contemporizing the former and universalizing the latter.

THREE STAGES OF SOCIAL GROWTH.

A TABULATION OF THE CONTENTS OF THE FOREGOING CHAPTER.

STAGES.	THE TYPICAL INDIVIDUAL.	BASIS OF SOVEREIGNTY.	FORM OF GOVERNMENT.	NATURE OF LAW.	PROPERTY AND ITS RIGHT.	LITERATURE.	RELIGION.
I. Society at one with itself. *What is, is.*	The naive laborer. Body and soul one. Society an organism.	The social life; the state and its members being identical.	Direct government. Cf. Patriarchism, the Greek city-state, etc.	Personal command. No written law.	Land and its products. Common ownership. Barter. No selected medium of exchange.	Ballads, folk-lore, myths, etc., communicated through word of mouth.	Naturistic, simple. God and nature one, and very near to man.
II. Society alienated from itself. *What is not, is.*	The soldier. Body and soul two. Society a physical mechanism, a spiritual community.	Worldly might and spiritual sanction or divine appointment. Separation of state and individuals.	Absolute monarchy. The monarch as the universal individual.	Statutory, positive, based on tradition. No equity.	Domain and coin. Abstract or universal; unworldly. Right in possession. Freely inheritable.	Scriptural, ready-made. Language, the lifeless repository of a fixed truth. No active thinking.	Supernatural, revealed. Manifest in a single book or in a single man.
III. Society restored to itself. *What is, is.*	The mechanic. Body and soul one again. Society an organism.	The social will; the will of society as a self-conscious organism.	Representative, democratic, constitutional. Constitution definitive, not creative of society.	Mediative, adaptive, based on equity.	Machinery and credit. No separation of capital and labor, of will and action. Freedom of transportation and communication.	Living, mediative. Thought and life inseparable. Language a living function of environment.	Natural, but from the supernatural being naturalized. God immanent in humanity.

CHAPTER X.

THE PROCESS OF SOCIETY'S ALIENATION FROM ITSELF.

NOW that we have the landmarks of a society's progress so well defined, we can follow the course of it in greater detail. The processes of alienation and restoration that make the transition from the first stage to the second and from the second to the third respectively are most important, and by the continuity or self-consistency that will be manifested in them, will help to make the real significance of the stages themselves still more definite to us.*

Of the first of these two transitional processes we have already had at least a general view. In a very general way we have seen how social individuation involves territorial and historical and industrial consciousness,

---

*Recall, too, from above this statement: "The peculiar relation between the sequent and the coexistent that the conditions of activity [or progress] evidently require makes continuity as that alone in which the two can be at one with each other a necessity. Continuity is only a purely physical conception of relationship." Pp. 29-30.

conflict with self or nature, rising formalism, disintegration at home, and abroad hostile relations which threaten invasion if not overthrow; but there are important accompaniments of these general changes which should have careful consideration.

Social individuation, very much like personal individuation, induces an organic localization of functions. It brings a more or less definite, an ever more definite division of society into distinct classes, and a more or less definite, an ever more definite localization of these classes in the recognized territory. Of course the territorial separation of a society is evidence of an organically differentiating and localizing process in the life of nature as the including whole, and this is a fact not to be lost sight of, but for the present it is to be kept in the background. For the present we are to narrow our view to the inner change and condition of an individual society. What, then, a society's inner differentiation—at once political and geographical—is and why it is are the problems confronting us.

But these problems are easily solved, for social individuation, like personal individuation, involves an intensification of consciousness, a growing tension in the expression of the organic life; and with this a society begins to divide the labor of its activity and particularly to develop within itself certain special organs or classes, whose office it is to define the consciousness, and certain other special organs or classes, whose office it is to supply the more material needs of the social life. In other words, thinkers arise, who separate themselves from direct contact with life and nature, and servants or—in the narrower sense—laborers, who retain a relation to life and nature, but in such a lifeless or mechanical or left-handed way as to make them materially as well as formally the contemporaries of their leisured "superiors." And with this separation of classes there comes also the development of towns and cities and of a single metropolis or intellectual and political centre. In the metropolis the social life grows intense, keenly self-conscious, dramatic, more brilliant than genuine, while beyond the city gates, in what comes to be called almost reproachfully the "country," the life seems even to be losing the consciousness that it had, becoming dull, monotonous and quite as unreal as the glare of the distant city. A poet might exclaim of the two: Is not one the dull east, the other the glowing west of a closing day!

But a keener consciousness in an individual society, as in an individual person, signifies control or—to use a word familiar to the psychologists if to no one else—inhibition; and control or inhibition does not mean cessation of activity, but activity for its own sake instead of for any clearly recognized motive or relation beyond itself. Some time ago we found activity for activity's sake, the turning of life into a cult, a natural accompaniment of a society's conflict with itself, but now we are to connect it with the differentiation of society into classes both locally and functionally distinct. In order to act effectively against the strengthening opposition without a society must get itself together, whatever the cost; and, as we know, the cost is a growing self-consciousness with all its incidents. The cost is a consciousness that is as dramatic—or abstract—as it is local and an overt activity, a conduct of life, a labor, that is as mechanical as it is local. Only with this cost can the control, necessary to greater effectiveness, be secured. But why call it cost? Because it shows society living its own death, becoming alienated from itself.

Consciousness, then, signifies control; it signifies a control which on one side, that of the self-conscious, dramatic reproduction of life, is to be seen geographically in the city and politically in the leisured class, and on the other side, that of the mechanical conduct of life, geographically in the country and politically in the serving or laboring class.*

In a city, as it grows, we see a people coming to live its life as if to itself. The city, so wonderfully mobile, shows us miles of farmland and years of experience focussed in a single square. It is the very much contracted life, and its institutions are the very much contracted symbol of the country. The old relations of course persist, the old interests and the old needs, but wonderfully intensified.

---

* Of much that has been said and is yet to be said in this chapter, I have already given a rough outline (*Dynamic Idealism*, pp. 190 sq.), and except for occasional verbal changes I may at times even quote myself literally here without the encumbrance of quotation marks. At the time of the earlier statement I was chiefly interested in using the process of social change as an illustration of the general process of thought. The process of thought manifests a similar functional and spatial differentiation. In company with the definition of consciousness, thought-organs are developed that are distinct from the organs of conduct, and also in company with the developed expression of thought in language there appears the distinction between right-handedness—or conscious activity—and left-handedness—or mechanical activity. The visible institutions of a society are the language in which its thought is expressed.

The great department store, for example, is the country store over again, but on a much grander scale; and the streets have the same functions as the country roads, but driver and wayfarer cannot be too alert. Yes, the city repeats or dramatically rehearses the country life, and intensifies it, turning simplicity into complexity, naiveté into self-consciousness and sophistication. But, more than this, the rise of the city, with its congested population and all, shows the country life suffering decline, for the people as a whole are living to themselves, as if the activity were for its own sake, not to nature. Consider how the rural civilization decays. The country folk lose their culture and change to mere drudges, little better than day-laborers, living with nature perhaps, but not to her; living—as said before—only left-handedly. Inactivity sets in among them. Their agriculture passes into the hands of large owners and becomes—so far as they are concerned—a purely mechanical process. Possibly it is taken from them altogether by being transferred to unsettled territory, or by being assumed by the cheaper labor of invaders. And the city's great department store not only reproduces the country store, but also takes away its business by conducting an ever-increasing out-of-town trade. The city, too, goes to the theatre and the ball, while the deserted folk on the neglected farms pine for the days when life was so much more worth while, even resenting the means of communication and transportation that have made the changes possible. In short, then, the country dies as the city lives; and it dies, just because —as was said—in the city a people is living its old life to itself, the more positive expression of it having been put in abeyance. Or, again, with its absorbing interest in control, in distribution and communication and manufacture, rather than in direct production, the city manifests just such a withdrawal from nature— from the sphere of original expression—as is implied always in the rise of self-consciousness; and the country—that is perhaps more beautiful or more picturesque by reason of the decay —in its dull existence shows the contemporary effect on the conduct of life.

But somebody is impatient to accuse me of forgetting myself. In what purports to be an account of a much earlier time in the life of human society I am allowing myself the most modern terms, terms that are so modern as possibly to seem even vulgarly offensive to those who have any proper historical sense. I am like the great preacher who thrilled his audience with the roar of cannon and the glitter of bayonets in one of the long-ago battles between Romans and Parthians. Well, I confess my forgetfulness; but what historian, who ever gets free from mere antiquarism, can help forgetting? A modern realism surely does no greater violence to history than antiquarism. Terms indeed may change in the course of time, but the relations of life do not change. Besides, have we not found that the contemporary past was the only past that we could recognize? Whatever we may call them, the things that are were and the things that were are. A physical scientist sees the same law, the same force, in both the explosion of gunpowder and the blows and movements of battle-axes and javelins, and an economist the same social life in both the marts of ancient cities and the great department stores of today. So my forgetting is also remembering.

And, turning now to the political in distinction from the geograpical differentiation of an individual or self-conscious society, we shall get still more history of the sort that finds the past also present. Thus, the control or inhibition that the consciousness brings shows itself also in the so-called supremacy of the leisured class. The thinkers rule; the laborers obey. There is, too, a third class, as if to mediate between these two extremes, that is in general the official class. The thinkers define in the social consciousness the law of the social life; the workers preserve the life itself while the definition is in process; the officials execute the law as it is promulgated; and all three are at once functionally distinguishable but materially contemporary. Simply a society become self-conscious and awakened to the pressing need of control can do without no one of them.

It is often said that a thinking or intellectual class arises in society whenever prosperity has brought leisure, and this statement is true enough when it is properly understood. One needs first to recognize that leisure in one direction always brings severe responsibility in another, that there may be, nay must be as much leisure in labor as in thought, and secondly to comprehend fully what the dependence of a leisured thinking class on a serving laboring class really is. The thought-life, however abstract its thinking may become, is based psychologically as well as sociologically on what in general we are calling labor. Is it not an incident of control? And is control less easy than expression? Thinker and laborer are born of the same social life, and what the former controls in spite of the tendency of his nature the latter expresses without the need of thought. Which, then, has the most leisure, the inactive thinker or the unthinking laborer, it would indeed be hard to say. But, furthermore, in regard to the relation of the two, the relegation of the labor of a society to slaves or servants or to men of material affairs generally, which is so necessary to the rise of an intellectual class, never takes place and never can take place unless *all* have the acquired power to do what is relegated to the few. Are not all, as was said, sprung from the same life? Thinkers and laborers alike must have a developed capacity, a freedom, which in terms of powers and impulses is the same, even if it come to overt expression only among the latter; and in this freedom, in this acquired capacity, although inert or only potential in the life of those that think, lies the real basis of the intellectual life. Thus, to repeat summarily, the subjective capacity to do the work of society and the relegation of the work itself to a special class are equally necessary to the rise of thinkers, the former being a psychological and the latter a sociological condition. There were no thought, no science, possible in a social life without labor, and the thinker as well as the laborer must have the power, the adapted structure that the labor requires. How else could thought define to society the law of its activity? Why, even the circus-performer, what with his great skill in expressing the relations of space, is one of a whole army of servants of the abstract sciences of space and motion; but no man on earth could be an abstract mathematician who was not structurally adapted to move in space as freely as the most agile gymnast. This is a fanciful, if not an absurd illustration; but I think it embodies a principle. In the gymnast, as in all cases of service, we see a certain activity taken out of real life and made a cult, and this abstraction is only as it were the open practice of that which an abstract science defines. Moreover, the science and the practice, which are equally abstract, must be remembered as the two intimately related incidents of the control that a self-conscious society finds necessary; and while they are both of them signs that society is being alienated from itself, they are signs also, because of their intimate relation, that alienation is not all that is going on. Psychologically or sociologically, the time can not but come when labor and thought will return to each other. Thus, whenever science is afield, it is well to look for a revolution. But this is anticipating.

A society's thought is long in developing and we need to follow the process of the development in its several moments before we can adequately comprehend how it must culminate in a revolution. That alienation is a forerunner of revolution is quite evident, but the successive details of the process are important, although their differences may prove to be only in degree. Accordingly, with reference particularly to the three social classes, already named, the thinkers, the officials, and the laborers, I have found it convenient to recognize five moments in the alienating process, these moments, namely: (1) the moment of consciously asserted patriotism; (2) the moment of æsthethic self-appreciation; (3) the moment of the cosmopolitan spirit; (4) the moment of assumed and cultivated naturalism, and (5) the moment of spiritual surrender and resignation. Thus, here they are in a table, with the contemporary class changes:

FIVE MOMENTS IN A SOCIETY'S ALIENATION FROM ITSELF.

Order of Moments.	Thinkers.	Officials.	Laborers.	Historical Illustration.
1	Law-makers.	Public guardians or patriots.	Slaves.	Greece before Pericles' time,
2	Artists.	Conscious and critical citizens.	Paid servants.	The age of Pericles.
3	Scientists.	Politicians.	Artisans.	The period just before Socrates.
4	Philosophers.	Fatalists or time-servers.	Revolutionists.	The Socratic Period.
5	Religious leader or monarch.	Followers or disciples.	Hirelings.	Greece a Christian-Roman province.

A mere glance at this table shows a progressive increase in the degree of the alienation of the society as a whole from itself, from its institutions and traditions, or—otherwise put—a progressive increase in the degree of the independence or individual freedom of the members of society. The very slaves are liberated, but only as their superiors, the thinkers and the officials, lose their own loyalty to the existing order of things. In the fourth column of the table I have introduced a set of illustrations from the past which are somewhat dangerous, but if used cautiously may be helpful. Also it is to be recognized that the names selected for the different classes in the different moments had to be selected somewhat arbitrarily. Naming the moments of a continuous process is exactly like naming the indistinguishable parts of the spectrum. The unity of the table, however, will help to interpret the parts of it. But let us follow the different moments in detail.

In general thought controls activity in order to unify or organize it, and in society's unification or organization of its life the first thinkers to arise are naturally law-makers, because law is a means to the mere control rather than to the positive interpretation of what is doing. Mere control, through legal "thou shalts" and "thou shalt nots," is an antecedent condition of interpretation, or rather of *clearer* interpretation, since the control itself, when possible, is evidence of a more or less indefinite sense of what the interpretation is going to be. In individual experience, when conflict and need of adjustment come, we at first treat ourselves legally—do we not?—issuing commands to ourselves to do or not to do this or that which in themselves are not interpretations of what we are doing but both imply interpretation and lead to more definite interpretation of what our life is and so of what ought to be its expression. Law-makers, then, being the first thinkers, slaves as those who in their obedience are as unreasoning as the law that controls them are the first laborers, and public guardians or patriots, by whom the law is confused with the state or who are almost blind in their loyalty to the law as well as in their treatment of the slaves, are the first officials.

And after law, art. Both law and art are material or sensuous in their terms and in their standpoint, but law interprets and controls the impulses of life only implicitly, or say negatively or indirectly, while art interprets and controls them directly and positively. Art does not say: "Thou shalt" and "Thou shalt not," but simply reveals unity or harmony in the sphere of the expression of the different acts to which man is impelled, and this unity or harmony exercises control. The control, however, is no longer arbitrary or irrational, being as much a matter of motive as of command, of will as of compulsion, and as if in recognition of this change, the laborers in society become paid servants, servants who have a conscious and voluntary share in the unity of the social life, and the officials become conscious citizens in the sense of observers and critics of what is doing rather than mere unreasoning champions of it. Every part of society has to share in the change; else the artist's consciousness would be in the air and he would have no public.

That art is more alienating, or more liberating, than law hardly needs to be said. Art transfers the control of life from the human to the natural and so subordinates human law to natural law, or—as the same thing—finds a principle of control in human experience as such. Human experience includes nature as well as man, and when treated as the source of that which controls man it tends to free him from the visible traditions and institutions of the society in which he has been living.

The rise of art in Greece illustrates this, and the rise of art at the close of the "dark ages'—accompanied as it was by the doctrine of justification by faith, that is only an appeal to human experience—also illustrates it; but here we shall speak only of the first. In Greek art, which came as a sort of celebration of Greek patriotism and achievement, we see a national life, its religion, its politics, and its morals, put upon the stage or in general held up for rational observation—and for criticism, since observation involves criticism.

"In the art and literature of Greece," if I may quote myself,* "it is wrong to see a people only paying tribute to its past. Art always defines the past, and definition of the past sets the future free. . . . . . In Greek art . . . there was more than a golden age, there was the closing in of a people's conflict. The expression of experience in works of art did for a time make the pulse beat faster with pleasure and sense of worth and power; but in the end the effect of putting the time-honored ways and long-cherished ideals and noble deeds and heroes upon the stage . . . . . was to show where the battle was yet to be fought, in that it heralded an age of rationalism as successor to morality and piety and patriotism. Staging life, however reverently at first, had to lead in time to moral laxity, impiety, corruption in political life, and general social disintegration. It robbed life of all that had given it worth and coherence and power to satisfy the moral and religious nature; it made the

* Citizenship and Salvation. pp. 14-15.

traditional meaning of life external; it turned life into a form or convention instead of a content with any substantial spiritual worth; into a something merely to be used . . . . . rather than what it had been—an inner strength and support. In the Greek plays [and they show the tendency in all art] natural law . . . came to succeed the gods [and also men] in the control of human life."

In short art alienates. In it, from the standpoint of the life out of which it springs, there is a motive to treachery. The control that it induces is lawlessness also, but only because natural law must always transgress the laws of men.

But after art, science. Science is art at its limit, very much as art might be styled legislation at its limit. Science sees only the natural, forgetting the human in so far as this is anything distinct; and, as a consequence, art's sensuously expressed ideal becomes only an idea or a natural mechanical law, the unity or harmony of art having become freed from any sensuous relation to restrained impulses or stimulating objects. The symbol of a scientific idea is a mere symbol, valueless in itself, being as indifferent to the purely sensuous consciousness as the external nature whose law it symbolizes; and the idea itself is an abstract idea, a concept. The difference in general between art and science is that between a real or living metaphor and a dead metaphor. Thus, science succeeds art in the life of a people so soon as the environment, which comprises the numerous institutions and customs of the social life, is turned to a dead metaphor, the life itself becoming formal or conventional. Indeed it might be said—in recognition of the process by which metaphors die—that familiarity breeds the contempt which science always has for art. And so, contemporary with scientists, as the representatives of the other social classes, are politicians, for whom the social life is a carefully, a mechanically measured opportunity instead of a devotion, cosmopolitanism having succeeded patriotism and æsthetic satisfaction, and artisans, who also serve a trade instead of a master. Perhaps cosmopolitanism—it will be remembered that we characterized this third moment as that of the cosmopolitan spirit—is not the right word for this place, but it can err only in being perhaps a shade too explicit or too advanced, for in the naturally laissez-faire attitude of science and the disloyal selfishness of the politician and the dependence of the artisan on his tools, on his application of nature's resources, the spirit of cosmopolitanism is certainly more than merely implicit.

Succeeding the scientist is the philosopher; and with the philosopher come the time-server or fatalist and the revolutionist. These terms have been perhaps the hardest of all to select, but each one of them is intended to indicate the final assertion of independence of traditions, institutions, and long-cherished ideals. Science, although not materially loyal to the existing order, is still formally so, and the politician and artisan are naturally conservative in the same way, but the philosopher and his contemporaries lose even the form of loyalty to what is. The fatalist does but execute the law that the philosopher makes and the revolutionist, as enemy abroad or traitor at home, does but obediently practice it. In them all the society to which they belong has brought itself to the level of the life without. Through conquest, perhaps—as with the imperialist Alexander the Great—or finally through submission—as when Greece became a Roman province—the leveling, which is identical with alienation, fulfills itself.

And conquest or submission, or let us say imperialism, in which conquest and submission are identical, changes philosophy into religion, thought into faith, the naive individual that had been, at the beginning, into the soldier as the typical character of the second stage of a society's activity. But why?

Just because the alienation is so complete. The philosopher's thinking ceases to be his thinking, or any body's thinking, almost as soon as it has found expression. The philosopher's thought is nature's thought; his reason is a world-reason. For him, even while he speaks, nature ceases to be even formally external to man, becoming all-inclusive, all-absorbing. To him man and nature, the subjective and the objective, the inner and the outer, the life at home and the life abroad, neighbor and foreigner are one. Through him the spirit of the age, both as a thought and as a life, is set free, or rather through him thought and life are made one. But the unity of thought and life, upon which the freedom of the Spirit of the Age really depends, is religion; it is religion in the sense that identifies faith and works.

Science, we saw, was art at its limit, and in like manner philosophy is science at its limit. As was said, even the only formal separation of subject and object, upon which science depends, disappears in the thinking of philosophy, so that—and this involves the truth of all limits, does it not?—philosophy, although the limit of science, is itself not scientific. The limit outgrows its antecedents. And with the outgrowth expression of the thought of a society is no longer even in lifeless institutions, in environment as a dead metaphor, in abstract formulae, but is embodied in the life of a man who is the incarnation of the thought that had begun in society so long ago and that is at last set free and who comes to a people which is still blinded by its own dead traditions as the messenger of another world, although he is but the revealed motive of their own history. So, again, philosophy is a forerunner of religion; a forerunner of the return of complexity into simplicity, of the return of man to nature, of the fall of cities and the death of abstract thinkers. Is not philosophy agnosticism or skepticism, and being this can its conclusion be anything but faith and simplicity? When man is at one with nature must not the word become incarnate?

But what have conquest and submission to do with all this? What has imperialism, in which conquest and submission were but just now said to be identical, to do with all this? Why, the motive to conquest shows the life without conquering the inner, does it not? It shows the beginning of a surrender of an isolated individuality. Alexander, already mentioned in illustration, did indeed carry Greek civilization to the barbarians, but not less did he alienate the Greeks from themselves and prepare the downfall of their civilization, of their art and science and religion. After Alexander the Greek became a barbarian, or Greek and barbarian, as if man and nature became one in imperial Rome. And the power of Rome—had it a worldly or a spiritual sanction? It had both in one. The monarch was also the God, the Incarnate Spirit of another world, and his subjects, at once soldiers and disciples. So, then, is the alienation of a society from itself fulfilled in imperialism, the establishing principle of which, I should say, is this, that belief in another world as supernatural, by being a corrective of a people's isolation or partiality, is liberation of the natural in this.

Certainly the physical, the natural, is never so supreme as when the supernatural is recognized.

Here, however, we are in danger of encroaching upon the concerns of the next chapter, while there still remains something to be said upon what is at present before us. The process that we have been examining, in which a society is seen to become alienated from itself, was said at the very beginning of our examination to be a measure of defence. To meet a recognized danger from without society develops thinkers and founds cities, thereby focusing and intensifying its own individuality. But is this sort of defence effective? Historically, yes. It made Thermopylae and Marathon, Salamis and Plataea, possible; and it finally brought the Greek face to face with himself. We need, in a word, to remember that the defence, although at first sight of civilized man against barbarian, was—and always is—in reality of human nature against man or even of nature in general against herself and that the final victory comes only when a people can say with Socrates, who saw so deeply into the truth of alienation; "To die is gain."

And, finally, in the succession of social classes we must not for a moment imagine that the old classes disappear as the new arise, although in a qualified sense it is true that they do. The old thinkers, for example, always persist, but in subjection to the new. When art has succeeded law, law itself appeals from the human to the natural, losing its purely mandatory character, and when science has succeeded art, art becomes formal and mechanical, and philosophy turns mystical with the advent of religion, and corresponding changes occur in the relations of the classes contemporary with the thinkers. Cities, moreover, in their development so intimately related to the changes in the social classes, really include the country. Has not somebody compared a city with a great octopus? But here a reminiscence or two: History ever transcends both its stages and its localities by persistently contemporizing the former and universalizing the latter; and: Progress is the contemporizing law of the past, whether as thought or as environment, becoming the motive, which is only the contemporized future, of the all-inclusive present.

CHAPTER XI.

THE PROCESS OF SOCIETY'S RESTORATION TO ITSELF.

WHAT *is not*, *is*, was the highly technical formula that we ventured to give for the second stage of a society's progress and it was the formula of the very imperialism or supernaturalism or absolutism into which we have just seen a society to pass upon the completion of its alienation from itself. The belief, however, in another world, in a supernatural world, appeared as a corrective of partiality of life in the world that is, for it only liberates a freer, a more general and more fundamental expression of the natural. So, at the very moment of complete alienation restoration is assured. Liberation of the natural can not but restore an alienated society to itself.

But let us look even once more to the state in which a society finds itself at the moment of its extreme alienation. Here it is, although somewhat differently put. The end of life is wholly apart from the means. In terms of popular usage, the means is physical, the end spiritual. Living creatures being responsible to the other world instead of to this and so being the mere medium of a physical process, are become the tools or in their social unity the tool of whoever among them has gained the greatest physical power. They are the means or the source of the power, but their spiritual abstraction, implying as it does a perfect physical or mechanical differentiation among them, sanctions an individual leadership. The leader as spiritually the universal individual is but the visible representative of all, and as physically the leader only takes his peculiar place in the differentiated mechanical whole. Society, in short, is an army that has life in the other world, not indeed for its motive, since then its individual members would be suicides instead of soldiers, but for its fearlessly recognized goal. The army, however, is not an army until it actually moves, motion very plainly being necessary to complete alienation, but also—and here we are to see how unreal the second stage, the stage of absolute alienation, is—motion, which is identical with what was above referred to as liberation of the natural, not brings but *is* the restoration of society to itself.

The implications, then, of the motion or activity of an army or social mechanism, of society, as it were, in another world and so under a monarchical military despotism, say—for example—of imperial Rome, are the special objects of our present interest. What is the effect of the activity upon itself? Upon the leader and the subjects? Upon the social life and all its manifold relations? What exactly is the nature of the restoration which the activity *is?*

Briefly, summarily, the effect upon itself of the activity or movement of a social mechanism is not only to reveal to consciousness but also to idealize or glorify its conditions. It is a very general truth—is it not?—that activity always glorifies whatever has made it possible. Nothing can be so real as to be liberative without also being ideal. But just what are the liberative conditions of a social mechanism? Of course they are without number, but all of them are reducible at least to two, namely, to differentiation of all the parts as the first and to a unifying relationship as the second; and in the motion which they condition or make possible even these two are, so to speak, brought into each other or fulfilled in each other. The differentiation proves to be identical with organization; the unity and the differences are intrinsic to each other. This, however, signifies that the spiritual as the one or the universal and the physical as the many, the different or the particular, are brought together, that the supernatural is brought down to the natural or the natural raised to the supernatural. In a word, politically—as well as psychologically—the free movement of a mechanism is *ipso facto* realization of an organism, since the organic is just that in which unity and difference are at once identified and idealized, or in which the otherness of the supernatural is naturalized, and this in turn is only to say abstractly what in the concrete we know as the natural evolution of imperialism into internationalism, of monarchy into democracy, or of militarism into industrialism. Only let an army begin to move and each dying part, through its share in the movement of the whole, discovers in its own peculiar individuality a worth that is commensurate with that of the whole; and such a discovery means, as said, internationalism and democracy and industrialism.

Hence, in history, the very moment of

Rome's imperial supremacy was the birth of modern Christendom. Rome's freedom brought her fall; not, however, in the sense of decomposition or disintegration, which is all that some historians have been able to see, but in the sense of organic differentiation. Rome's fall, in other words, was also her fulfilment. Her unity persists today, but transformed, because—as has been asserted in effect—the conditions of its realization became ideal at the very moment of its expression. Christendom has now and always has had for its rock, for its foundation, the principle that the other world, instead of being something wholly apart from this, is only a truth or a reality which underlies man's relation to the world that is. The other world, as has been said more than once, just by reason of its otherness corrects isolation or partiality; it effects or inculcates a responsibility to the whole; and responsibility to the whole, implying as it does that the whole is organically one, is and has been both the teaching and the practice of Christendom.

So the birth of the organic in the mechanical is our general account of the transition from the second stage to the third—or from imperial Rome to our own time—and with this general view before us we can pass to a more detailed examination of the process.

Thus, by no means the least important thing that we see is the rise of a distinction between the national—or individualistic—and the impepial—or universalistic—institutions in the life of society. Thus, state and church are differentiated; and king and pope, language and Latin, laborer and soldier, production and exchange, commodity and medium or standard of value, machinery and nature as mere domain, *jus civile* and *jus gentium*, science and religion; and so on indefinitely. This differentiation, moreover, has both a geographical and a political* expression, but instead of looking directly at these aspects of it we shall here take a more general view. First, however, a caution is necessary. In each of the pairs of terms enumerated some one may see only a distinction without a difference and turn upon me with the very pertinent question: Which is national and which imperial? In each case I meant to put the national first, but I am not absolutely sure that I have kept the same standpoint throughout the enumeration,

---

*In the narrower sense of "political" as referring to differentiation of social classes.

and change of standpoint would indeed change the order, since—absolutely—each term in any pair is all that the other is. How could anything else be true, when the differentiation is necessarily an organic one? But just what I mean here, if it is not evident already, will appear as we proceed.

The differentiation of state and church is one of the most familiar incidents of the fall of Rome, and from the standpoint of the church it meant two things, the loss of the temporal power and the rise of a spiritual—as well as of a temporal—apostasy. Society became ever more and more independent of the church as an institution, justification by faith supplanting justification by ecclesiastical mediation; and, although the Roman Church remained intact it lost its hold upon all in society except in general the ignorant and unskilled and indeed retained its authority over these only by adapting itself to the new conditions. The history of confession and indulgences is a startling record of preservation through adaptation. But in spite of losses and changes through Protestantism the Roman Church has been and still is the visible representative of an imperial or international religion. There may be the motive to unity among all peoples in the churches and sects of Protestantism, for they too are separated from the State, being concerned not with the political but with the human, but whatever their inner spirit they are still rather national than imperial, while Romanism stands out as the *manifest* symbol of the imperialism of Christianity.

The differentiation of king and pope, of course involved in that of state and church, is—or was—plainly in the interest of nationalism, or rather, as indicative of both the differentiation and organization, of internationalism, the king representing the individual part and the pope the whole. But the king is never the arbitrary ruler that the Pope—or Emperor—had been. From the beginning he is responsible on the one hand to the Pope as the head of the original whole, and on the other hand to the life of his people as that upon which the individuality, that is due to the differentiation, depends. Moreover these two sources of the responsibility are in reality not two but one, for as the latter materializes the other turns merely spiritual or formal. Witness the translation of the Pope from emperor to political figure-head, from worldly to unworldly sovereignty, from imperial domain to virtual imprisonment. But, to return, the monarch over the separated part of an original empire is necessarily a limited or responsible monarch, and very early in the development of the European nations the kings or monarchs were looked upon as bound by laws of nature or principles of humanity, the Pope being for a time the administrator or executor of these laws or principles or being—let us say with the same meaning—the source of International Law. International Law is in itself an appeal to the human or the natural, as Hugo de Groot realized at the beginning of the seventeenth century. And which of the two, Pope or King, is national? Which imperial? Well, in answer I should say, what was implied of church and state, that each is invisibly what the other is visibly. They are both related, mutually determining incidents of an international life.

Of the rise of national languages and the accompanying decline of the imperial Latin it is not necessary to speak at length. Of course Latin still has a place, but only as a part of the ritual in the Roman church or as an educational discipline throughout Christendom; and in either of these functions it shows the imperial turned formal in the interest of the national or individual. And as for the national languages it is sufficient to remember that they are organically one language, only reflecting in their relations and interactions the life of the nations to which they belong. They have never been dead to each other.

But the differentiation of laborer and soldier is an incident in the process of restoration that is of special importance to us and it calls therefore for a most careful treatment. The limitation of monarchy that rises with the organic division of the imperial whole is naturally accompanied by a check upon militarism; for, should the old militarism persist, the division could not be real, the assertion of national and personal individuality could be only imaginary. In fact, no separate part can even will a return to the career or the standpoint of the whole, since to will the repetition is to will its own destruction. Simply, the original expression changes the meaning and will is always loyal to meaning. Yes, I know, that at one time there was thought of reestablishing the Roman Empire, but what historian sees therein anything more than at best the repetition of a name? Repetition can not be literal; it must be evolution also. So, to continue, the assertion of individuality—whether national or personal—being coincident with the realization of a positive share in the mechanical process of society under an empire, is inseparable from the development of mechanical skill in the individual. Moreover, it is certain that the mechanical skill so arising will be applied to just that upon which the differentiation or the individuality depends. And upon what is the individuality dependent? To what does it owe its content, its substantial reality? Certainly not the human, as at the time conceived, since in terms of this alone society is an army, not an organism. What then? Why, the natural or the physical. With the organic division of empire the asserted individuals must turn, nay, they have already turned for expression to their peculiar environments, to their peculiarly natural resources. Their individual consciousness has its objective source in a nature that is not human in so far as it differentiates each one of their number from all the others. Accordingly, instead of mechanicalizing the human they mechanicalize the natural; and in doing this—let us keep in mind—they are only applying the skill, as if an inheritance, which their origin in the imperial army insures to them. Mechanicalization of the natural, however, differentiates not only one individual from others but also, specifically, the laborer from the soldier, the skilful, self-active individual from the individual that is only the passive medium of a mechanical process. The laborer as member of the society that ensues—whether of personal or of national individuals—is the agency, through which the future, and the soldier, through which the past is contemporized with the present.

Are illustrations necessary? Necessary or not, they are very plentiful and as diverse as plentiful. The confessional as it becomes mechanical develops the conscience of the penitent, who becomes himself a master of the ecclesiastical machinery and applies his skill to experience in general. A habit of mind once established is always freed from the special sphere of its training. Religion, furthermore, as it becomes doctrinal or dogmatic, by inculcating a sense of lawfulness as such, makes science not only possible but inevitable; like Rome in her relation to Spartacus, arming and training an enemy. Monarchy by its very absoluteness becomes democracy, since it has to let the people into its secret. A teacher who has a system proves to be only a part of a mechanism which his pupils use skilfully. And, in general, whenever living creatures are subjected to a mechanical process they invariably turn upon the process itself and use it to their own individual ends. Always mechanism realizes organism, in the general sphere of the animate relating the living to the inorganic and in society the human to the natural or the civilized to the uncivilized. But the relation must be understood also as both a widening and a deepening of the living or the human or the civilized. Thus, to return to the illustrations, Spartacus as enemy of Rome is no longer a slave; the Christian, turned scientist, is not Catholic but Protestant; the obedient subject of a monarch is already a voter; and the wide-awake pupil shares in the teaching.

So, again, the organic division of empire with its limitation of monarchy and its check to militarism brings the separation of laborer and soldier. Military service is relegated to a special class, the "standing army." The soldier, however, ceases to be what he had been, since even as a soldier he can not but be the laborer's contemporary. He really turns laborer himself, being employed by society to do a particular thing and being in his military service at least as much concerned with his wages as with the service itself or being henceforth more than a mere soldier. Peace instead of war is the object of his maintenance. In brief, then, although visibly he is a sign of the original imperialism, he is also a nationalistic or individualistic factor in the social life. To read the history of the "balance of power" in Europe is to see the struggle of an organic nationalism, an internationalism, to free itself from a persisting imperialism.

But, the soldier aside, it must not be supposed that society suddenly acquires the individual person as a laborer with mechanical skill. The personal members of the empire are long in securing their heritage, for the division begins with nations or classes rather than with persons or at least *retrospectively* it seems to begin so; so that it can be said with almost scientific exactness that in proportion as the classes are large in size and few in number the power over nature is slight and the expression of it more dependent on the toil of labor-armies than on natural or physical machinery, while in proportion as the division reaches the personal individual the power over nature is great and its expression in a mechanicalized nature. The history of feudalism shows this. Industrialism, beginning with the beginning of the division of Rome, is seen to be a development from a simple agriculture and a very crude sort of manufacture or from a condition of labor-armies or labor-guilds dependent less on individual skill than on organization to a condition in which even agriculture is elaborate manufacture and in which manufacture in general relies on skill and most complex machinery. Of course, although not always appreciated, the simple industry of the earlier time is not without some conscious measurement of natural resources— witness the early systems of rents and all the laws or customs that define in any way the position of the laborer—and such measurement always implies some mechanical adaptation of physical force, but in comparison with later times—except as it illustrates what has been asserted here—this earlier mechanical skill is almost insignificant.

The conscious measurement of natural resources, mediating as it does between the human and the natural, is an important incident of the differentiation of soldier and laborer, which we have been neglecting. We had a momentary view of it when we saw that the birth of organism out of mechanism involves the birth of individual consciousness and that this consciousness as it rises relates the subjective and the objective, the human and the natural, but we need to look more closely. As implied already, the measurement, the consciousness is at first in classes rather than in individual persons; or, if in individuals, it is in these as monarchical leaders, not as persons; and this can have no other effect than to make the thinking of the time a purely deductive one to the persons themselves. A formal logic, too, has the place of objective science, formal logic being not merely the linguistic or grammatical logic of scholasticism but in general the abstract study of any mere medium of expression. Politics and theology and finance can be quite as scholastic as the formal logic in the narrow sense. Thinking in classes, or—to recall a school-day memory—"in chorus," and abstraction of the medium of expression and deduction as the ideal reasoning are but three sides of what is a strictly equilateral triangle. But, as a matter of course, induction is not lacking even here, since the classes themselves and the consciousness give evidence that individuality has already asserted itself in subject and in object alike. Moreover, to issue again a well-worn caution, the past in which we find a deductive logic, a class-thinking, and an external medium, is only as we see it. This, however, does not make our observations any less worth while. It only enables us to comprehend them better. Absolutely, consciousness is always at once inductive and deductive, although, if we study history, we have to find the sciences developing from the deductive to the inductive. Historically too —and it is chiefly to this that I have been coming, since it is so important in an understanding of the relation of industrialism to militarism— we can not recognize a consciously inductive and objective thinking until the organic division of empire is seen to have reached just such a personal individuality as we assume for ourselves. Thus, the dimensions of Christendom and the self-consciousness have not changed materially since Descartes on one side and Bacon on the other formulated the method to which individual thinking still adheres.*

*In other words, to put the truth of the paragraph differently, thinking, or consciousness, is always both social and individual. Compare the discussion of the social consciousness, p. 109 ff. But historically the thought-process is always seen as from the past and social to the present and individual or as from the deductive to the inductive.

But adequately to understand the evolution of the personal laborer we need to go still deeper. The conscious measurement of natural resources upon which expression of mechanical skill depends is nothing more nor less than the application of mathematics to physical phenomena. So long, however, as thinking is deductive and government monarchical, the mathematics applied is mensuration rather than anything else, a mathematics that is not much better than a rule of thumb. Just as politically one person is made the standard for the judgment of all others, so scientifically one particular thing as an abitrary unit is taken as the measure of everything else. Only as thinking becomes personally individual and inductive and objective is a pure mathematics or a pure mechanics possible.* To show just how this is, in the space that can be taken here, is not easy, and yet the truth of it is familiar to all students of history and an historical truth never can be in-

---

*Kant—is he the last Roman or the first great modern philosopher?—finds the three primary concepts of mechanics, space and time and causality, only the *apriori* forms of the individual's objective experience and so reduces all true science to a pure mechanics. Space and time and causality, however, are also only very general or let us say *naturalistic* names for the attributes or prerogatives of sovereignty. Space is domain; time, the unity of national self-consciousness, and causality, executive power.

capable of explanation. Moreover, the explanation which we seek seems to be in the fact that the mathematician, as such, is as imperial as individual, his principles being not less his than everybody's, or that the object studied in mathematics is always a universal individual. Exactly the typical individual, which an inductive natural science struggles after through all the subtle device of its experimentation, mathematics or mechanics has before it from the beginning. Mechanism, always subject to mathematical description, in nature at large as well as in human society presupposes a universal or an imperial individuality.

Should any one ask me just what the mathematician's imperial individual is I should be disposed to reply that at least the best representative of it is the infinitesimal. Certainly no concept has done more than this to make a pure mathematics or a pure mechanics possible. The infinitesimal is the individual freed from any arbitrary or particular content and by dint of its freedom is as imperial or all-inclusive as individual. In mechanics infinite and finite are all but if not quite identified, and at the risk of seeming extravagantly fanciful I must confess to finding, as well as to believing that any conscientious historian will find a world of meaning in the parallelism between the development of the identification of God with nature and that of the identification—in mathematics—of the infinite with the finite. Bruno, the Cartesians and Spinoza, who are only the thinkers of their times bringing to consciousness what their fellows effect unconsciously or unreflectively, do for theology exactly what their contemporaries, Kepler and Galileo and Newton and Leibnitz do for mathematics; they discover the other world in this, the divine in the human and natural, the infinite in the finite. Remember, too, that the effect on human society of the conception of the other world as spaceless and timeless,* as wholly immaterial, as strictly a negative of this, is to justify militarism or social mechanicalism and that only as the other world comes to be found in this is the individual set free in an organic social life; and, remembering this, reflect that by what is more than a mere coincidence the differential calculus so fundamental to mechanics and treating the infinite as intrinsic to the finite is a contemporary not only

---

*Obviously the infinitesimal is spaceless and timeless too; as a quantity it is zero itself.

of democratic institutions, which define society as an organism, but also of biology, which has the organic for its central idea. In the monad of Leibnitz, moreover, we see and he seems to have seen at once the infinitesimal of mechanics and the organism of biology. So, as was suggested before, religion—not theology—is the inspiration of science. It may seem fanciful to interpret history in this way, but certainly it is well worth while.

In our discussion of conscious measurement, of deduction and induction, of mathematics and of the infinitesimal and the monad we seem to have lost sight of the laborer as a person mechanically skilful; but he returns to our view as soon as we recall from the preceding chapter what was found to be the relation in society of the laborer and the thinker. In society's experience and progress the thinker does but define what the laborer enacts. The skilful mechanic is the serving contemporary of the science of mechanics; he is a psychological as well as a sociological condition of it. Why, feeble indeed is the thinker who can not read the industrial individualism of Adam Smith in the monadology of Leibnitz.

But, in conclusion of this rather long discussion of the separation of laborer and soldier, of the birth of industrialism in militarism or organism in mechanism, we have now to add to the several incidents already considered the ever greater freedom of communication and transportation between the different parts of the imperial whole. By what means is this freedom secured? Necessarily by the same means to which the developing individuality owes its reality; that is to say, by the mechanical application of natural force. It is justice indeed that exactly what makes the individuality possible makes possible also the communication and transportation, in other words, the commercial exchange, which the individuality requires. Am I thinking of the telegraph and the locomotive and the printing-press as naturally contemporary with cotton-gins, with looms and spindles, and with all the complex machinery of agriculture and manufacture? As a matter of course. Locomotive and press, cotton-gin and the others are extremely concrete, it is true, but they have their place in the philosophy of history. Are we mathematicians? Then we can see in them the miraculous infinitesimal through which we have been able to transcend the finiteness of space and time. Are we economists? We see in them the imperial unity of industrialism, to which also belongs the same transcendence of spacial and temporal limitations. They do but insure to the individual laborer both his individuality and the imperial sovereignty that he has as his lawful inheritance from the soldier. They give him an imperial as well as an individual consciousness and an imperial as well as an individual activity. They show how right we were in thinking of the other world, the infinite, as but a principle in this, a corrective of isolation and partiality.

And now we are ready to turn to the separation of production and exchange, which was also mentioned above in evidence of the rise of the distinction between the individual and the imperial institutions of a social life. This particular separation, moreover, being plainly identical with that of commodity and medium or of machinery and mere nature,* we can consider all three together. Under an extreme militarism the bank, which controls exchange, and the factory,** which controls production,

---

* In machinery and mere nature any technically informed philosopher can not fail to see the phenomenal world of scientific experience and the thing-in-itself of Kant.

** In the sense of any instrument or institution of manufacture in general.

must be one and the same institution, for treasure or mere domain can be the only form of property and possession can be the only basis of the right of property, production in the sense of manufacture having no place. Domain is only the sphere or one might almost say the repository of treasure; and the treasure—through the vicissitudes of history—may include slaves and works of art and literature and other evidences of a past civilization, but its most natural or logical form is the precious metal, which is a very typical part of nature as mere domain and is valuable because natural and relatively indestructible and freely transportable and unlimited by any of the special pleasures or interests of mankind. As coin the precious metal is as abstractly universal as the other world itself in which its owners are virtually living. Such production, then, as there is can consist only in getting and in keeping treasure or the domain that contains it or particularly in getting and in keeping coin; and with production so conditioned bank and factory are indeed inseparable and physical force expressed in an army is the machinery with which both the banking and the production are carried on.

But the conditions of militarism are its own overthrow. The movement of the army relates the other world to this and with the relation the army begins to disband; the soldiers as soldiers die. Whether we think of Rome as converted to Christianity or of her subjects as surfeited with worldly treasure, we see her fall; we see the disbanding, the differentiation of her social machine; we see the other world brought into this, Heaven turned earthly and worldly treasure turned really useful to man and nature turned positively productive: and through such changes factory and bank—very much as state and church—are separated, and with them commodity and medium, and machinery and nature.

Of these changes, interesting as they are, I hesitate to speak in much detail, partly because I have already discussed them at considerable length in another book,* but chiefly because I do not find the detailed discussion of them necessary to my present purposes. Still I must add a little to the foregoing, for there is one circumstance, connected particularly with the separation of medium and commodity, that is of peculiar interest. That the bank as a

* *Citizenship and Salvation*, pp. 92-102 and 129-136.

separate institution is one of the vital incidents of the transition from the old militarism to the present industrialism is a well-known fact of history and that the factory has developed with the bank is another. The bank's function, moreover, is one of exchange among individuals either through its bills of deposit or through the loans by which it makes production possible, while the factory is the great agent of production; and each is, to recall a refrain, invisibly what the other is visibly. It is also equally well known to the historian that with the development of industrialism coin becomes valuable only as one commodity among others, while in its capacity of medium of exchange it approaches ever nearer to being a mere symbol or economic figure-head. Its transfiguration or translation is quite comparable with that of the political or ecclesiastical monarch contemporary with it. In finance, moreover,—and this is what I have had specially in mind,—the change is not without its conflict of dogmatism and heresy. Just as there is the conflict of ecclesiasticism and atheism and of absolutism and anarchy so there is that of metalism and fiatism;* and as always in cases of conflict the

---

* Is this a new word? I am not sure. Of course the reference is to the heresy of "fiat-money."

right is on neither side. Religion, for example, is neither orthodoxy nor agnosticism but the faith that is also works; the natural sovereignty is neither in a personal monarch nor in the separate members of society but in the life of all as a social life; and similarly in finance the real medium of exchange is neither a precious metal, however stable, nor a bit of paper, however stamped, but what the business world knows as credit—credit of the sort that really "turns the wheels of industry." So long, then, as militarism persists, threatening or positively encumbering the life of an industrial society, the dogma of metalism will persist too, and with it the heresy of fiatism, but the very conflict of these two, involved as it is in the development of a free industrialism or in what we have been calling the restoration of society to itself, is the earnest of a genuine credit becoming the medium of exchange.

In an organic freely industrial society productive power, not possession, constitutes the right to property. So long, however, as any particular commodity—even gold!—serves as the medium, there remains some right in mere possession. But credit becoming the medium alters the case materially. And exactly what is credit? It is not something that can ever be hoarded. It is not something that can ever be lent. It is certainly not any bare say-so. What then? It is a medium of exchange *and of nothing but exchange.* It is financial or commercial intelligence. It is the social consciousness—which is as individual as social—of the productive capacity of the social life.* For credit to succed a metal or metals as the medium of exchange a prompt and accurate communication is necessary among all the parts, however distant or however rural, of the commercial world; and the bank, not as a treasure-house, not as an institution merely of loans and deposits, but as an institution that operates only in credit instruments and the intelligence on which they are based, must be available to every part and every person of the social whole.

Am I understood here? If I am, a perfectly logical connection will be evident among these different things that follow: geographical centralization, arbitrary class-distinctions, irre-

* Credit, as here defined, is to be associated closely with machinery. The two are but the inseparable aspects of an industrial life or, as Spinza would have put it, the parallel attributes of one substance. Credit is industrialism on the side of mind or thought; machinery, on the side of matter or extension.

sponsible personal leadership, artificially protected capital, ignorant and unskilled labor, dogmatic when not heretical metalism* in finance, communication and transportation that is neither socially nor geographically general and that is inaccurate or insecure as well as incomplete, corrupt politics, and—not to extend a list that is of indefinite length—abstract or laissez-faire science. Certainly a remarkable jumble! And to it might be added a sectarian time-serving religion, a sensational machine-controlled newspaper, a social code that in public and in private takes the will for the deed and so sanctions incapacity in office and sentimentality in morals generally, and literal** inheritance both of social position and private character. But I was not to extend the list. In it, however, we have a veritable photograph or rather a photographic "negative" of our own time; as it were, the system of shadows cast by the light of society's restoration to itself. And in it we have also a summary history of Christendom.

* Heretical metalism has fiatism for its limit. Of course dogmatism is always a justification of heresy.
** "Literal" inheritance is the inheritance of a persistent character or status, of a character or status that continues in the offspring to be *literally* what it was in the parent.

But as further evidence of the development of the distinction between individual and imperial institutions in the social life, a development that we found coincident with the process of restoration, there were mentioned above, as will be remembered, two other cases of differentiation, the case of *jus civile* and *jus gentium* and the case of science and religion. Of these, however, nothing more can be said here. Science and religion are to be treated in a separate chapter; and the history of jurisprudence must speak for itself, although I might add to the illustration given the simple fact that the development of equity, as distinct from the common law, is contemporaneous with that of international law. Both equity and international law make one and the same appeal. They appeal, not to the traditional or socially conventional and instituted but to the widely human and natural. Accordingly they serve organism instead of mechanism in the relations of men.

Finally, there are certain incidents, not yet referred to, of that special phase of the process of restoration which has been called here the naturalization of the supernatural, and to these we must now give some attention. Thus, as not the least important although possibly the least obvious among the unnoticed incidents of the naturalization of the supernatural, there is barbarian invasion. In history we see barbarian hordes overcoming Rome almost at the moment of her conversion to Christianity, and so preventing her Christian idealism from becoming idle and abstract or unworldly. At just the time, when the church has been separated from the state* and has completed its organization and systematized its doctrines, the barbarians appear, as if the messengers of nature or—shall we not say it?—of God himself, to insure usefulness or application. The Imperial City has the thought and the will; they supply the necessity and the force. The visible Rome, already in decay, they easily overcome; while the church masters them, yet not without adapting—and this means naturalizing—its machinery. The adaptation, moreover, or the naturalization ends in Protestantism; or—more strictly—the invasion itself is the beginning of the Protestant Reformation, the barbarian invaders, even at their conversion to Roman Catholisim, being the first Protestants.

*Conspicuously by the division of Rome into an Eastern and a Western Empire.

And, if invasion brings naturalization and Protestantism, learning, in spite of its cloistered seclusion—and literature and painting—in spite of their sacred subjects—and architecture—in spite of its limitation to places of worship—and pilgrimage—in spite of its destination—bring them also. All these, moreover, are the means the church finds necessary in its career of conversion and adaptation; arguments, I like to call them, when I try to comprehend the reasoning in the eomplex all-inclusive history of Christendom, from the natural to the supernatural. And they are certainly very effective arguments, being of the sort that justify by fulfilling without idolatrously perpetuating what they would defend. Also in what might well be called the return of Greece and Judea, in the influx of Greek scholars and the revival of Greek learning and in the rise to prominence and power of the Jewish banker, we see not only an effective argument from the natural to the supernatural but also a movement that makes the process of society's restoration to itself seem almost a literal one. To use Milton's words, Greece and Judea are "lost" only to be "regained."

Protestantism, moreover, in the end awakened

to the full force of its own arguments and so become a necessity of the personal consciousness, declares in all the ways of its expression that, since human experience is the only justification, the other world must be here and now; and in realization of this declaration, in fulfilment of all sorts of prophecies of the millenium and satisfaction of all sorts of political air-castles America takes her place as an organic part of Christendom. The invasion, that has naturalized Catholicism, Protestantism turns into exploration and discovery, and in history no argument from the natural to the supernatural is more telling than this of the discovery of America. In the discovery of America, too, not more for what it has realized in the new world than for what it has brought about in in the old, we have most positively expressed— for what but this have we found democracy and industrialism and liberty of belief to signify?—the restoration of society to itself.

CHAPTER XII.

PROGRESS IN THE ACTIVITY OF SOCIETY.

ALIENATION and restoration, traced in the last two chapters as altogether distinct stages in the life of society, are in reality like Heraclitus' "way up" and "way down." They are "the same." Indeed the dark philosopher himself may be imagined to say of them that in the fire of social progress each is as a back-log to the other. Were the relation less close, were they in any way separate, the progress of society could never satisfy the demands that our thinking has made upon the conception of progress. Simply, progress is not genuine if not both conservative and radical.*

The intimacy of the two processes was manifested to us in the fact that the same agencies could be appealed to in explanation of them both. Thus, the art of Greece alienated; the

* Here it can hardly be necessary to say, because virtually it is to reiterate, that in general only the activity of an organism, in which unity and difference are identified, can be both conservative and radical. For an organism to be is to progress.

art of Christendom restored. Art, however, and all the other expressions of society's reflection upon the social life always both alienate and restore; they must ever do one in doing the other. The art of Christendom has certainly revived a life that had seemed dead. restoring an earlier civilization to the consciousness and activity of the present, but also and with no less truth it has brought a rationalism and a criticism that are alienating Christendom from itself. Moreover, at risk of seeming only verbally gymnastic, we need to add that the alienated Christendom has been taking the restored Greece and Judea with it, so that it is as if the past's rebirth were the present's death. Has not the self-consciousness of Christendom made both Greek history and Jewish history essential to Christian history, and in doing this has it not also given both Greek and Jew an *active* share in the life of Christendom? To face our paradox boldly, the old, the long-ago, is not dead but lives in the new, while the new dies as the old revives.

Frequently it is said that history repeats itself, but that is not what I am saying here. What thoughtful person would say of a runner that in his successive strides he was constantly repeating himself? No race is a series of repeated strides and no history, or no evolution, however rhythmic, is a series of repeated "moments." Any movement, that of racing or that of human progress, is an absolutely indivisible whole; what we may choose to see as the action of a moment or a part is in reality all-inclusive; and, this being true, to speak of repetition in the runner's race or in man's history is to be even worse than thoughtless. The present never repeats the past, for the past is a related part of the life of the present. What is memory, forsooth, but a peculiar consciousness accompanying certain disturbances in a body that is all together and all at once?

How can I make myself clear? We are so accustomed to divide time into intervals, and in the intervals to see a series of successive processes, that any other demands upon our thinking are grossly fanciful if not hopelessly unintelligible. They seem to promise nothing but paradoxes, and to many paradoxes are as stones when bread is wanted. But paradoxes, like stones, have an important rôle in human life. Thus, as regards the present discussion, we have found another than a composite divisible time in which to read history and in spite of the paradoxes that it leads us into the new reading feeds our thought. In time, as we have found it, there is always a backward as well as a forward movement or quite without the verbal contradiction activity is always organic differentiation. Any process of the present, then, notably the social movement of Christendom, must be as if filling the time of all human history.

And here do but revive some of our earlier general conclusions. "The life of the present and the life of the past are wrongly thought of as two lives. . . . Not those that are now gone once lived and we live, but they and we are living; they in us and we with them." "Life or action in its temporal sequences is but the continuous expression of the persistent relations of coexistences." The individual—person or nation or civilization—is a "vital relation," an "organic function," that "transcends any mere bounds of space and time" and that "has an immortality that is as substantial and inviolable as the universe itself."

Restoration, in the light now upon it, is not far from being equivalent to the organic recapitulation of the past. It is the process by which the past is related to the present and changed as the relation demands. And alienation, in its turn, is the organic anticipation of the future. The two, moreover, mutually dependent and inseparable as they are, do but show that contemporization of past and future with the present which we saw to be so essential to a truly progressive activity. Yes, they are stages or moments of progress, as already they have been treated here; given a particular ideal or standard to determine one's judgment, as when one has regard to a particular history, for example the history of Christendom, and they are bound to appear in a temporal series; but they are always contemporaneous as well as successive, one being always active in the other. Day and night could not be more truly both contemporary and successive than they. In short, then, as has been asserted here so often in one way or another, the new is not less alive in the present than the old; as in walking, so in human history, so in the evolution of life generally. Everywhere the activity that is also progress reaches forward and outward at the same time that it reaches backward and inward. Advance always involves a *present* animation or more specifically with reference to human affairs a *present* civilization at once of the prehistoric past and of the lifeless or uncivilized or shall we not say the post-historic future; it brings into recognition and more vital expression what had seemed temporally and spatially external. When has human progress been without both a new consciousness of an ever earlier civilization and a developed sympathy for still uncivilized parts? Progress seems to mean realization of the future through glorification or at least justification of the past. What, for example, has meant more to Christianity than its discovery of a pre-Christian existence? And, with regard to what is spatially external, it was surely the more inclusive life of the Mediterranean that so intensified and deepened the life of Greece and Judæa as to set them quite beside themselves, and today it is a more inclusive life that is alienating Christendom.

Here is not exactly the place for prophecy, but there seems to be a general agreement that the future of Christendom is in some substantial way to involve the life of the un-Christian Orient, and the reasons are many for attributing the present alienation to the Eastern Question. This Eastern Question, it is not necessary to say, is and always has been a concrete condition as well as a question, a living relationship as well as a consciously formulated problem, and besides being political it has been also economic and psychological and theological. Christianity came from the East, and with it came other gifts. Perhaps, then, it is not so extravagant, as it may seem at first, to imagine that the East, taken for what it has meant both historically and geographically, both spiritually and materially, is the cause of the lights and shadows that we found in the conditions of our present life. The sense of isolation, the consciousness of unfulfilled responsibilities, always makes both lights and shadows, and it is certain that no one in the Occident has been free from such a consciousness since the beginning of the Christian era.

But I may get mystical, if I go on. True, there are times when clearness is a fault. Enough, however, if in the complex phenomena of history which we have been studying we have found presented to us only a wonderfully magnified illustration of what progress is—"the timeless because defining and contemporizing law of the past, whether as thought or as environment, becoming the motive, which is only the defined and contemporized future, of the all-including present." Confessedly, a rather forbidding formula, and it does not improve much with its repetitions, but after all, as we often say of our uncomely friends, "handsome is that handsome does."

Part III.
HISTORICAL STUDIES.

CHAPTER XIII.

REASON AND RELIGION.

THE lights and shadows that mean alienation or restoration, according to the direction of our looking, and that somehow, let us say because of the necessities of vision or the laws of optics, prevent our undivided attention in either direction, are nowhere more striking than in the relation of reason and religion. In fact it would not be difficult to reduce all history to what is sometimes called the conflict between the two, and if history were so reduced the life that is would naturally appear in the same form. For religion and reason—what are they but action or impulse and inaction or consciousness? And their conflict—what but that between impulse and consciousness?

Reason is sometimes identified with science. It is, however, as used here, a more general term, being synonymous with thought. Science we have found to be but one moment in a process of thought—or reason—that has control, or inhibition, as one of its incidents and activity merely for activity's sake as the other and that expresses itself politically in the development of distinct classes, notably the leisured thinking classes and the mechanically living working classes and geographically in the rise of an urban and the decay of the rural civilization. Other moments, as will be recalled, are legislation, art, and philosophy, science coming between the last two. The conflict of reason and religion, therefore, or of science and religion, begins with the beginning of this process, with the appearance of a thinking class and the development of the city.

But, furthermore, it must be kept in mind that those two incidents, control and activity for its own sake or mechanical activity are not strictly two but one essentially, being functionally or organically related. Each of the two is psychologically and sociologically a condition of the other, and in this unity they really give evidence of the rise among the people of a life, an activity, that promises to relate the people intimately and positively to what at the beginning they imagine is quite alien to them. Thus, in course of time, the thinkers lose their patriotism and the city even avows cosmopolitanism; the laborers pass into socialists of some kind and the country becomes the home of foreigners. In other words, the conscious control and the mechanical and relatively unconscious activity for its own sake, which makes the consciousness possible, are themselves for the sake of the more inclusive, the deeper and the broader life that is inducing the change. At first, as was said, the people may view their abstract thinking and their mechanical living as means of mere defense, but gradually and inevitably there arises a more positive interest in what seems to be opposing them and with this their treachery, which is also something else, asserts itself and the self-consciousness and conventional living give way to the new life.

And what has religion to do here? Well, I must repeat that religion, which has to do with action or impulse, and reason, which has to do with inaction or consciousness, come to be distinguished in the social life only as country and city or as labor and thought are distinguished. Religion identifies itself chiefly with those that work. Geographically it has its stronghold in the rural districts.* Religion and reason, then, must be organically one, sociologically and psychologically dependent; and the moments in the development of religion must be thoroughly sympathetic with those in the development of reason. Thus, religion must move, and the historian knows that it does move, through ecclesiastical polity and æsthetic ritualism to "rational" theology, while reason passes through jurisprudence and art to exact science, and in either case the process is one of alienation. Moreover, when the two have reached their third moments, society begins to feel and comes in course of time to say that religion is not rational theology or that the religious life is not ecclesiasticism, and that reason or thought is not abstract science or science only for science's sake, and with this awakening religion is seen to turn "liberal," keeping the letter but affirming only the spirit, and science to turn "positivistic," keeping the formulæ but only as "working

*That I am here making the case simpler than it really is I am well aware, but I am hardly likely to be misunderstood. The distinctions that I make depend on differences of an organic life in society, not on the exclusive or isolating differences of a merely composite life. Religion has its own thinkers, the theologians, just as science has its own laborers, the mechanics, and religion and science are also geographically coextensive.

hypotheses." In short, a motive to philosophy is in the consciousness of the people, and there appear in society, as if visible exponents of the change, religious spirits, who have as their ideal the application to life itself, to social conditions, to human needs, of scientific ideas or principles. These pioneers, however, who are independent alike of the church and of the school or university, are doomed to fail partially, when not wholly, in their longing to bring impulse and consciousness, religion and reason together, for on the one hand they lack the necessary machinery and on the other the necessary understanding to make their labor effective. They are would-be reformers, the laborers or servants of philosophy, but the society to which they belong, being still at least formally orthodox and conservative, damns them and hinders them by finding them irreligious or even atheistic and unscientific or even cranky and quack. Perhaps nothing shows the alienation of society from itself so emphatically as this appearance of non-religious—or non-ecclesiastical—religion and non-scientific—or non-academic—science. It is, moreover, as we know, an earnest of the last moment in the process of alienation, when alienation is manifestly restoration; the moment of religion and reason, impulse and consciousness, identified; the moment, in a word, when change or even revolution or—shall we not say?—transfiguration comes, not exactly to the life of society, but to the body, to the institutions.

The foregoing sketch, rapid and concise as it is, suffices to show that the conflict, so much talked of, is not of religion and reason but of theology, which is religion alienated from itself, and of science, which is reason alienated from itself, and that the alienation in either case is a perfectly natural incident of a society's struggle with itself, of the tension of a society's effort at expression or adjustment. In justification of this too much emphasis can not be laid on the unity of spirit, the formal unity, which has been indicated, of the two opponents. Unity of form or spirit in the contestants is really a law of all conflict. Thus, to add to what has been said above, as regards theology and science, both are rationalistic; both are dogmatic; both would have it that their formulae or creeds are ends in themselves; and both are abstract and unsocial, professional and institutional. The liberalism which passes into a virtual agnosticism of the one is quite in line with the positivism of the other. If one is only sentimental in what it does, being so spiritual as to be thoroughly material, as when charity is confined to gifts of money, and is in consequence as likely to do harm as to do good, the other is at the same time cold and indifferent, or *laissez faire*, and so from its side quite as harmful as helpful. But, agreeing so remarkably in all these ways, how do they differ? Only in visible content; in the architecture of their buildings, the personnel of their followers, and the matter of their preaching. Some one objects, bidding me to remember, among many other things, the wide difference, spiritual as well as material, between the doctrines of Christianity and those of evolution. I have to reply, however, that it is not at all fanciful to read the doctrines of orthodox theology in those of evolution or of science generally.* Spontaneous genesis is only science for creation; genus or species is only science for church or sect; and chance for miracle, the exact law or formula for the intuited dogma, the force-endowed

---

*See an article in *The Monist*, Jan., 1899, "Evolution Evolved—A Philosophical Chriticism;" also, in *The Philosophical Review*, July, 1898, "Epistemology and Physical Science—A Fatal Parallelism."

atom or the vital unit for the soul-endowed body, and so on indefinitely. So, implicitly or metaphysically, the teachings of science and the teachings of theology are not essentially different, however wide apart they may be externally. But the external, the material difference—does it amount to nothing? Of course it amounts to something. It makes the conflict real, the formal unity being that which makes it only possible; or rather the formal unity and material difference show how each of the opponents is as much in conflict with itself as with anything outside. How else explain the dogmatism of the one or the positivism of the other? The inefficient activity of the one or the efficient inactivity of the other? The cloistered and scheduled ritual of the one or—what shall I say?—the physical exercise of the other?

And the conflict of theology and science, whether with themselves or with each other, only shows how a society as well as an individual person must always look before it leaps. The conflict is the looking. Impulse keeps its traditional motives—hence the dogmatism of theology—until science becomes really applicable, and thought has to be equally out of touch with reality, equally formal and abstract, until its own accuracy has changed it from knowledge into motive. But let these changes be realized, and action is freed from mere doing, from mere ritual, and identified with thinking, and thought from mere science and identified with action; the word becomes incarnate.

But science is the limit of art, and in view of the undisputed intimacy between art and religion it is worth our while to see in just what way art persists in science. Curiously enough art and science never seem fully in sympathy with each other, the limit appearing to outgrow its own origin. The difference between the two is closely parallel with that between man and nature, the subjective and the objective. Science would eliminate the human altogether, and so be literally objective or naturalistic. When all is said, however, science is by no means so far from art as it often imagines itself. Thus, as all agree, art objectifies human life or human experience, putting its achievements on the stage of consciousness, dramatizing its struggle and its victories, exposing it, and revealing in it a law or a will that is superior to human law or human will, but does this in material that is either visibly human or sensuously, subjectively stimulating to the human; and science also objectifies and dramatizes human life, but in the natural. Science sees men as animals or even as mere bodies; society as only a genus or species, or as a group of atoms or molecules; activity as mere natural life or even as physical motion ; and death as only so much change. Science, then, is art with a microscope. The laboratory is its theater; the report or contribution, its novel or its poem; the diagram, its painting; and the equation, which literally reduces everything to nothing, at once its comedy and its tragedy. But being art at its limit or art with the distinction betwen man and nature or subject and object become the merest convention, science fails to find even a suspicion of personality in the superior will or law that it reveals. Art is always teleological, creationalistic; but science recognizes and realizes the implied fatalism, preserving what is at best only a formal teleology, regarding all that is ultimate as absolutely unknowable.

But, finally, art is the new transcending without surrendering the old; a radical conservatism; lawlessness persistently lawful; cosmopolitanism or naturalism remaining patriotic or humanistic. This is art, and science is its last word, its dying message. Rational theology, then, contemporary with science, is also the last word, the concluding rite of a sensuous ceremonial. And thought and religion, being each real because in and of the other, follow quickly; the new becomes free and active; the human identifies itself with the natural, with the world-reason, and through the identification finds the natural personal.

So we make reason religious and religion rational. The two are one in the Incarnate Word, which restores or redeems man, while it changes or even destroys his political and geographical devices.

CHAPTER XIV.

GOOD AND EVIL.

HISTORY may be seen also as a conflict of good and evil; and, if history, then the present too.

Sometimes this conflict is regarded as between distinct forces or beings, sometimes—more abstractly—as between the spiritual and the material, sometimes as between the human and the natural, sometimes as between different classes of living creatures or still more narrowly of human beings, but no one of these numerous views is adequate to the conception of history at which we have arrived. All of these are but one in this respect. They make the good and the evil separate and independent and turn the conflict into one of either annihilation or exclusion, whereas from our standpoint history, which is the liberation of activity in its own realized law, can admit neither the annihilation nor the exclusion of any one of its incidents. Conflict that annihilates or excludes is meaningless to us.

And equally inadequate to our conception of history is the notion, not uncommon today, that the good and the evil are wholly relative to times and conditions. As usually understood this is only another way of making the conflict meaningless, since it makes the good and the evil themselves unreal or unsubstantial.

But, if the good and the evil are neither self-existent and absolute nor relative, what can they be? Indeed is there any third view of them open to us? There is this possibility. The *distinction* between the two may be real and substantial, being a necessary incident or a necessary experience of all activity; a real incident, then, or a real experience of all life. Is this consistent with history as the liberation of activity in its own realized law? It certainly is. History, so conditioned, can never be free from the tension of a lawful expression of itself, from the conflict of the good as lawfulness and the evil as lawlessness. Moreover, just because the mere expression of activity must always bring a clearer consciousness of its conditions, the lawful and the lawless, although always significant can be neither absolute nor relative. In fact lawfulness, when for its own sake, is become lawless and lawlessness as independence of mere convention is lawful. The two, in short, are always necessarily distinguished, but neither of them exists by itself or in mere antithesis to the other. They are the differentiated conditions of a life or an activity that, being indivisible, gives to all of its conditions mutual dependence and determination. They are neither absolute nor relative, because themselves a relation. Of them, as we see them opposed, we have to say that each is invisibly whatever the other is visibly or—in another formula which is directly applicable to the distinction of the good and the bad in society and which is also getting to be one of our refrains—that each is psychologically and sociologically dependent on the other.

Here we shall have to confine ourselves to the conflict of good and evil as a social phenomenon, although whatever is said can not but be applicable *mutatis mutandis* in natural science as interested in good and evil in nature or in psychology and ethics as interested in good and evil in the personal individual. Society only mediates between nature and the individual.

In the first place, then, the consciousness of evil or, as indicated above, of lawlessness, is natural to a progressive social life for the reason that a life, whose expression defines the knowledge of its conditions, can not fail to discover evil in itself; and this consciousness has the form of condemnation or resentment. A progressive life is ever condemning itself. The evil, however, is evil only as it is discovered; it is evil only with the retrospection. The condemnation, too, is never without approval also, the despair over recognized evil never without a sense of good. A life that knows its evil is inherently, it is already actively and materially good.

But true as this is it must not for a moment be understood to mean that either the approval or the condemnation is of specific activities or ways of expression, for under all the conditions no way of expression, whether as manifested in an individual or as manifested in a particular group or class, can be good or bad in itself. No way of expression can be so independent of the changing life as to require either restraint or cultivation for the sake of anything intrinsic to its isolated self. Let us not forget that the liberation of a society's life in its own realized law, not the loss nor yet the addition or the mere perpetuation of any particular thing, is progress. Condemnation, then, and approval are both formally and materially inseparable and complementary phases of the consciousness that life induces and that would make life ever more at one with itself, ever more consistent, ever more organic. Even with regard to the objects upon which they are directed they are mutually inclusive, they are coextensive.

This is hard to understand, but to the historian there is the very clearest evidence of it in the way in which the two opposing classes of society, the good and the bad, the law-abiding and the lawless, literally involve each other. Only a short time ago it was remarked that lawfulness for its own sake, which is just what makes the distinction between the consciously good and those who are said to be bad, is lawlessness, and that lawlessness, separating the consciously bad from the good, is lawfulness, but a much more direct and perhaps a much more sensational way of saying the same thing is that what is good and what is bad in society are never under any circumstances to be identified with separate social classes. In a society that is an organism all are good together and all are bad together. The distinctions of classes mark, not a conflict merely of separate parts with each other, but a conflict rather of each part with itself or of society as an organic whole with itself.

The illustrations of this almost if not quite startling truth are both numerous and convincing. Thus, such in society as identify themselves with a *laissez-faire* science are evil to those who are identified with ecclesiasticism and theological dogmatism. The theism of the latter finds only atheism in the former. But it is an old story to us that each is whatever the other is, that the two are organically one, being mutually determining incidents of the same life. And, under precisely the same conditions, a silver-heresy is evil to a gold-orthodoxy, or in general fiatism to metalism; pleasure-seeking is evil to asceticism; reckless, unskilled labor, to thoughtless and masterful capital; adultery, to marriage under the law; murder, to hanging; gambling, to revelation and miracle; thieving, to business "honesty;" talent, to genius; leisure, to industry; theory, to practice; "Christian" science, to material or "physical" science; profanity, to cant; barbarian, to Greek; Jew, to Christian. Simply the life of society can not bring or involve these differences without having them dependent on each other and intrinsic to each other. When in history, political or economical, theological or moral, have the good in society condemned the bad without finding themselves condemned also? The good are indeed the saviours of society, but only as they find its sins in themselves. And when have the bad approved the good without finding themselves approved also? The bad do indeed share in the salvation, for a self-condemned society always forgives their sinfulness and takes them to itself.

That the law-abiding are parties to the transgression in the life of society and the transgressors to the lawfulness is an idea that is too true to the spirit of our times not to be recognized and accepted as soon as it has been clearly stated. Aside from the fact that ever since Christ was declared to have saved his fellows by taking their sins—idolatry, for example, murder, dishonor of parents, and adultery—upon himself and glorifying them,* society has felt with a growing keenness that responsibility both for the evil and the good is social as well as individual, it is interesting to

* Witness the divinity, crucifixion, ministry, and immaculate conception.

reflect in how many ways the social classes today that live in the law are recognizing and confessing their actual participation in the deeds of such as offend and how the offenders are even making claims to righteousness. Why, saviour and malefactor are as dependent today, as much involved in each other or as necessarily associated, as at the hour of the Crucifixion. What malefactor has not saved his fellows by taking their sins upon himself! And what wonder that the life, the social function of the malefactor became idealized!

Yes, to the malefactor, the transgressor, there belongs a function in the life of society, which is commensurate only with that of the leader or reformer, and the truth is that no fact needs to be appreciated more fully than this by the philosopher who would understand history. Surely real leaders are transgressors always. The very authority or sovereignty of a king lies in the principle that he "can do no wrong;" and, just as a king has to be exempt in this way, so a pope has to be infallible, a political leader irresponsible and arbitrary, and even a god licentious or miracle-working. Some centuries ago the notorious House of Stuart saved puritan England; and in all ages lawless gods have made their sinful worshippers lawful.

Now whenever extremes are made to meet, as we are here making the transgressor and the reformer meet, it seems at first as if life were losing its very foundations. Who has not had a sense of unreality upon learning that at best cold and hot differed only in degree? In the end, however, the meeting of extremes is found to establish instead of overthrow. Thus, to be able to see leadership or reform even in transgression is to make the life of mankind anything but hopeless, even in its worst conditions. The reformer appears as one who does but apply ideally or reflectively the natural function of the transgressor; he sanctifies the breaking of the law. Hence his sympathy and charity for his offending contemporaries. And the transgressor only unwittingly, that is, naturally rather than morally or spiritually serves his fellows. What the transgressor does in fact the reformer does also in act. The transgressor unintentionally makes public the private life of his fellows, his crime being their vice; his thieving, to recall some examples already given, being an exposure or even a parody of their "honesty," or his adultery, of their lawful marriage, or his profanity, of their cant, or his murder, of their capital punishment; and so doing he reveals them to themselves and even by his punishment effects their self-condemnation. And what is this but unconscious leadership or unconscious reform? The reformer is only the idealized transgressor; the transgressor, as it were, made useful or brought under control.

And no conclusion from this relation of the transgressor to the reformer can be more significant than that which has really been in our minds all along. Neither the good nor the evil is a determined thing. Neither is the endowment, the original virtue or the original sin, of any person or class, of any act or any way of living. This is repetition, but I say again that in the case of the different acts of an individual or in the case of the lives of the different members or classes of society all are good and bad together. To separate the good and the evil is to justify the latter and condemn the former. Can a man divide his own life? The life of society—is it not organic?

That the appearance of the transgressor as well as the appearance of his natural contemporary the reformer is an incident of the alienation of society from itself all but goes without saying. Both transgression and reform are alienation. To this relationship, however, attention will be called in a later chapter.

But here we have to consider a fact that in its first statement may seem quite unintelligible and yet that does but afford an illustration of what has been said above. Thus, the conflict of good and evil is identical with that of the organic and the mechanical, or politically of democracy and monarchy; for the monarch, as already suggested, is both a leader and a transgressor. Indeed leadership with its inseparable incidents of transgression and liberation must be recognized as very much more than the life and authority of any single individual. It belongs to every member of the organic whole. "Any single individual" is *every* individual, or, exactly as democracy would have it, all individuals are monarchs. Democracy is only a universalized, a fulfilled monarchy. In it the monarch's, the leader's, the transgressor's function is everybody's. It would give to every individual person something peculiar to do, something upon which others must not encroach, something which is his right but their wrong; and this, because individuality, identical with leadership, depends on the assumption of some special activity in an organic life. Or, again, a truly democratic society cannot but be an organism, and the life of an organism involves what in the industrial world is known as division of labor, but division of labor means that in some one line, in some one relation to the whole, each laborer, each person, is monarchically and imperially supreme, being capable of doing no wrong therein and so redeeming his fellows for their own peculiar activities from the sinfulness of his.

So, finally and in summary, are the evil and the good not two but one; being two, only because society comes into conflict with itself, but one, because, in an organic society the separate parts or the separated activities are necessarily functions of each other, mutually dependent and inclusive, each being invisibly what the other is visibly.*

* Perhaps in a note one may allow himself to indulge in fancies. The imagery, moreover, accompanying thought processes is of peculiar interest, at least to psychologists, at the present time. Persistent, then, throughout these pages, and particularly vivid whenever I have come to recognize the organic relation of the implicit to the explicit or of the invisible to the visible, has been the image or the idea of the relation of light and darkness, day and night, in the earth's motion with reference to the sun. The good and evil, for example, seem to be one exactly as day and night are one. Of course for a monistic philosophy an analogy between the spiritual and the physical should be discoverable, and psychologically imagery is always more than mere imagery.

CHAPTER XV.

REVOLUTION.

REVOLUTION, so intimately associated with the conflict of religion and reason, or again with the conflict of good and evil, is the natural outcome of alienation. It is a forerunner of restoration. It is manifested evolution. It is a return to nature; the natural active in the human; the human lost in the natural and become a mere tool. It is at once man's restoration or redemption and the change or even the destruction of his political and geographical devices. In short, it is man entering into a new humanity.

Historians are disposed to look to France for evidence of the nature of revolution. France seems like the laboratory of a people that is over-fond of sensational experiments, of explosions and other startling changes. But what is to be seen in France underlies all life or all history. For example, politically, England and France are often contrasted as if they were such extremes as cold and heat, but as cold and heat are manifestations of one law to the scientist, so England and France can show only one process to the historian.

In general, then, the most obvious cause of revolution, if any one cause can be selected, is the formalism that comes with a society's alienation from itself. Formalism involves mechanicalism and mechanicalism always puts into the hands of society a tool, as if a club, with which to knock over the existing institutions. Witness the struggle, which it brings, between dogmatic unspiritual theism and atheism, or between purely conventional morality and sensualism, or between unpatriotic or only outwardly patriotic Bourbonism and anarchy.

Too much has been said already to leave the meaning here very much in doubt. Long ago we saw how the penitent outgrows the confessional and becomes ever more personally conscientious, and again how religion, turning dogmatic, gives rise to science, and how monarchy develops democracy; and in each of these cases is evidence of revolution; in each the past becomes a tool for the overthrow of the present; in each conventionalism or formalism appears as only the other side of lawlessness.

Conventionalism, or formalism, is traditionalism, the worship of the letter of the past, and the conflict of a revolution is just that of traditionalism, which idolatrously separates the past from the present, and idealism, which concerns itself with an wholly abstract future. But when traditionalism and idealism cross swords, it is as if each had found only a condemning exposure of itself in the other and in the outcome it may even be that the opponents change places. Traditionalism by the very abstraction that it makes, by its indifference to the present, sanctions change; so to speak, it lets nature take its course; and nature taking its course is the process, exactly, with which an abstract or irresponsible idealism identifies itself. Nothing is quite so significant to an understanding of revolution as the way in which even so violent a change as death, the death of sacrifice or the death of execution, is never without sanction from either side. Abstraction of either past or future makes death to the present something that is even to be courted instead of feared. The traditionalist already is in another world, while the idealist has not yet entered this.

Do I seem to make it a matter of indifference on which side in a revolutionary conflict one happens to be? By making the opponents so in agreement with each other, nay, so inclusive of each other, by showing them to be co-operative even in their opposition, do I seem to take all the meaning out of the conflict itself? If so, I have not been understood. Does the physicist give up his faith in resistance, in impenetrability, in force, or in motion, because he finds that action is equal to reaction? On the contrary the equation comes as a justification of his scientific faith, and in like manner co-operation in conflict makes conflict more real, not less real. When in history has there been a struggle in which justice was not as much on one side as on the other? The historian is constantly recognizing this. Forgiving enemies, however, by finding them justified, never makes the battles less significant, or less glorious. It only gives to all involved a share in the results, just as all had had a share in the inducing conditions. Conflict does indeed depend on differences, but the differences do not exclude each other. When battle is on, an organic life has come into open conflict with itself, and all are at once friends and enemies to each other and to themselves. No, I am very certainly not making conflict meaningless; I am making it real; I am making it consistent with a substantial progress.

But, lastly, does the conflict of revolution involve a resort to militarism? To me, confessedly, this is a *relatively* unimportant question, although others, out of regard to present day controversies, to present day aspirations, will think differently. There are many who have become fond of dreaming of "peaceful revolutions," who like, perhaps, to talk of an "industrial" as distinct from a military revolution, or find comfort in the cry "Evolution, not revolution;" but surely no thinker, or let me say no real worker can deny or even wish to deny conflict to the future. A "peaceful revolution" is not possible, and a future without revolution might as well be past. But it is possible, indeed it even seems probable, that militarism is passing away. Disarmament is no longer unthinkable, for our times are manifesting the development of noteworthy checks to the resort to arms. To enumerate these is hardly necessary, but here they are in part. Internationalism, democracy, industrialism are checks that are growing in effectiveness. War, too, is becoming too dangerous, and no one can doubt that the more terrible its instruments are, the less likely is their use. Then the changing views of property and the absence of undiscovered and unclaimed territory are other checks to warfare. So such as dream of evolution without revolution or of peaceful revolution may be concerned with a half-truth, but, whatever is in store for the military way of expressing force through human nature, there can be no doubt that there is conflict ahead; hard, earnest, revolutionary conflict; progressive conflict; conflict that can not fail to destroy because it will be bent on fulfilling.

CHAPTER XVI.

THE GREAT MAN.

AS this book draws to a close, it almost seems as if an explanation, I might even say a justification of the great man had been the motive from the beginning. Such influential writers as Herbert Spencer on the one hand and W. H. Mallock on the other seem to me to have either unduly belittled or fatally exalted the great man's relation to society and social growth, and in consequence I must regard it a peculiarly interesting and valuable service to history and political science to show what the relation really is. Possibly—and I am by no means insensible to this possibility—my own view may be found inadequate, but even ambitious thinkers have to take risks. Success is only for those who dare to fail.

So, to face at once the danger of failure, the great man is an individual; he is pre-eminently an individual; and his individuality must surely be true to the conditions of individuality in general. Thus, he must really share in the causation of the social life. His consciousness and his activity must be also the social consciousness and the social activity. He must be an application of force, peculiarly of social force, or—as the same thing—the liberation and individuation, the focusing of an activity actual in the social life. Furthermore, he must have for his motive exactly that upon which his existence depends, namely, a relation, an organic relation to the life that encompasses him. Repetition, then, or imitation can not at any moment, be his interest, nor on the other hand, whether in his consciousness or in his activity, can mere eccentricity, mere isolation, have ideal value for him. As just said, he naturally seeks an organic relation; he seeks the expression of just what he is; so that both unity and difference, both imitation and invention are controlling interests in whatever he does. And these are not two interests of course, but one and inseparable, since in life that is organic unity and differences are intrinsic to each other.

In earlier pages we came to the conclusion that for evolution or for history consciousness and life, or thought and action, whether in the single individual or in society, are not merely coextensive but also essential to each other, each being at once a condition and a result of the other, and we concluded also, with special regard to the incidents of social development, that conscious activity induces alienation. A people, in other words, in so far as active and conscious, is always in some measure beside itself, living another life than what appears at least to casual observation to be its actual life. There can be no conscious activity, no organic social life, if a motive to otherness, a principle of differentiation, is not present. Moreover this motive or principle, is no mere abstract sentiment. It is no shadowy unreality. It is no purely formal principle of logic. On the contrary, from the beginning, it is an activity as well as a sentiment, a concrete condition as well as an idea. It is an active social force which is as necessary to the life of society as the more conservative interest in self-preservation, since it brings, not mere preservation, but realization, fulfilment, evolution.

And what have individuality and greatness to do with it? Individuality and greatness are dependent upon it or may even be identified with it. Thus, in the first place, individuality and greatness are different, perhaps, but as already implied they are not different in kind;

and, in the second place, the individuality that is great belongs always to the time in a society's life when alienation is extreme. By a principle, too, which is not less psychological and sociological than logical, greatness tends to stand alone, to inhere in a single individual. The greatest man is the sole representative of the otherness, of the other life, that his fellows in the way of being beside themselves have come to lead. Do you ask why? Would you know the principle? Singleness, then, is necessary to free expression, to clear and complete revelation, to conviction. It shows, and only it can show the alienation to be at its limit. Is the alienation partial and only in process? Then there is a number of great men. Is it, on the other hand, complete? There is but one great man, a solitary but a convincing and a convicting witness.

But the othernesss that makes greatness like the otherness that makes individuality must be at one as well as at variance with the environment; the individual, and particularly the great individual, must somehow belong to his times even while he seems aloof; else, to say the least, a philosophy of history can have nothing to do with him and his greatness. How, then, can these two conditions be realized? To say that all organic life involves them is to speak truly enough and it is to say all that is necessary so far as the mere principle goes, but it is too much of a formula here to be altogether satisfactory. And hardly more satisfactory is the statement that at a time when society is thoroughly alienated from itself the alien character of the great man must, as a matter of course, be expressive of a perfectly genuine adaptation. This, too, is true and sufficient in itself, but we can be still more direct and still more definite. Summarily, then, the relation of the great man to his contemporaries is that of end to means, or of future to past.

This calls for explanation, but the explanation is at hand. As has been shown here, the process of alienation involves the development of formalism or let us say of a conservatism that is formal in exact proportion as it is conservative or merely traditional, and such a development shows the life of a people, or more strictly speaking, the institutions of all sorts with which the life has been identified, losing their ideal or intrinsic value and becoming the mere material instrument of a new life. Thus, to give an example already familiar to us, patriotism and political unity or continuity pass into cosmopolitanism and political disintegration, the people becoming utilitarian even in the regard of their state and its forms and institutes. A formal allegiance persists of course; it persists, until it is purely empty or formal, until alienation is complete; with completion it avows its treachery, throwing off the disguise. With completion, however, the great man also appears, being only the visible symbol or exponent, the active agent of the end to which the traditional life is the already adapted or developed means. So came Socrates to the Greeks, and Christ to the Jews.

Traditionalism is in effect treating the means to life, as if it were the end. It is then, acting in or for the future but looking at the past. In short, a sort of advancing backward or a disguised radicalism. Psychologically—and this is a most important fact—it prepares a people for some particular function or service in the larger life into which they are entering; for a function or service that they finally recognize and appropriate with the life of the great man among them. Witness the development of the Greeks, after the time of Socrates, into imperial soldiers, and of the Jews, after the time of Christ, into money-lenders and bankers. Alienation turned Greek traditionalism into militarism, and Hebrew traditionalism into banking.*

Besides putting the past into use, or say besides developing formalism and eventually making it instrumental, greatness realizes or anticipates the future. The great man is progress incarnate. He contemporizes the past and the future with the present. Being the fully defined, the revealed and the individuated life of his people, he both realizes their past and expresses their future in his own career. They become his followers, doing socially what he has done individually. The very nature of his birth insures the repetition of his career in the life that includes him, his revealed achievement necessarily becoming its motive.

And the great man as progress incarnate, as one in whom both the past is fulfilled and the future is anticipated, is a witness to will and motive and individual responsibility in history, in social evolution. Thus, to keep the supreme illustrations, Socrates showed the Greek vic-

---

*In *Citizenship and Salvation*, already referred to, I have developed the idea of the last two or three paragraphs and of several that follow, at considerable length. Hence my brevity at this time.

torious over himself *before* the final conquest by Rome, and Christ "took captivity captive." With such anticipations of history to testify against it determinism can get no hold upon the mind of the historian, and in general individuality is made synonymous with a genuine freedom or with a truly moral responsibility.

So we see the great man. He is the spirit of his people liberated and embodied, as they are separated from themselves; the master of their past; the prophet of their future; a veritable mediator, in whom alienation and restoration meet and are identified; in fine, the individual always pre-eminent and supreme.

But at least two things more ought to be said, and the first of these is that greatness—or genius—is not talent. Genius and talent are indeed dependent upon each other "psychologically and sociologically;" but, as even common opinion has always recognized, they are quite distinct. Thus, the Sophists and the Jews had talent, but Socrates and Christ had genius. Talent is conservative, traditional, lawful; genius is free. Talent is time-serving. genius, independent. Talent uses; genius invents. Talent formulates; genius discovers and reveals. Talent worships and follows; genius leads. Talent alienates; genius restores.

And, secondly and lastly, the greatest genius is a religious leader. This does but follow from all that has been said. Nay, it is a virtual repetition, for above we saw how logical, or how true to history Rome's identification of religion and leadership became. The monarch was also the God, the Incarnate Spirit of another world; and his subjects, at once soldiers and disciples. Jurisprudence and art and science and philosophy, the stages in order of the thought that accompanies a society's alienation from itself, have their great men, but also their great men are never without company. The number in the group of the great may diminish as the stages succeed each other and with the diminution the greatness may increase, but the number is never one and the greatness is never supreme till the alienation, which brings conviction of another world, is at its limit. When, however, the number is one, the divine is manifest in the human, the other world is brought into this.

CONCLUSION.

TO summarize the foregoing pages, in order to draw their moral, is all that remains for us to do.

Here, then, is the summary, unnecessary, perhaps, but not altogether without use. History is the liberation of human society, as an organism organically related to nature, in its own realized law. Realization of the law is through the development of individuals, nations and persons, with all the incidents of alienation and restoration, of evil and good, of science and religion, of talent and genius, that have been found to be involved. And the individuals developed are agents of a genuine progress, since the very essence of individuality is at once adaptation or fulfillment of the past and realization of the future.

And, as for the moral to be drawn, I can content myself with just a word or two. History is no mere logical scheme. It is no body of knowledge to be learned and recited. It is no entertaining story to be read and then forgotten or, if perhaps remembered, retained as but the tool of some teacher's trade or the ornament of some gentleman's culture. And, finally, it is no fatal process external to human passion and human will. But what is it then?

History is the experience, the very life itself, which we call our own. To adopt the familiar formula of the sages of the East: The history of human society—*that art thou!* Its past? No. Its future? No. What? Its living, all-including present.

INDEX.

INDEX.

Note.—The following index is intended to be rather topical than verbal, so that in many cases the literal words will not be found on the pages referred to.

ALEXANDER, 162, 165.
Alienation, 76, 125, 126, 134, 142, 143 sq., 155, 201, 204, 215,
America, 37, 44, 51, 73, 122, 127, 141, 200.
Antiquarism, 150.
Approval, 225 sq.
Architecture, 199, 217,
Art, 155, 157 sq., 200, 219.
Artisans, 155, 161.

BANK, 190, 193, 246.
Barbarian, 122, 198, 227.
Berkeley, 62.
Bruno, 187.

CALCULUS, 187.
Capital, 140, 142.
Cartesians, 187.
Catholicism, 174, 180, 198.
Causation, 37 sq., 46, 53 n., 55.
Chance, 25, 42, 217.
Change, 50, 53.
China, 125.
Christ, 79, 228, 245, 247.
Christendom, 79, 172, 184, 202.
Christianity, 51, 79, 127, 141, 155, 175, 192, 207.
Christian Science, 227.

Church, 25, 173, 198.
Citizenship and Salvation, 159, 192, 246.
City, 145, 147, 167, 212.
Coexistence, 29, 32, 46, 84, 129.
Coin, 135, 142, 191, 193.
Columbus, 37, 44, 51, 73.
Communication, 149, 189.
Condemnation, 225 sq.
Conflict, 56, 88 sq., 123, 216, 238.
Conquest, 165.
Cousciousness, 31, 61, 65, 72, 80, 87.
Consciousness, social, 109.
Contemporaneity, 15, 34, 40, 44, 53, 56, 85, 93, 128, 151, 179, 246.
Control, 86 sq., 146, 151, 211.
Cosmopolitanism, 126, 154, 161, 213, 245.
Country, 145, 147, 212.
Creation, 33, 38, 55.
Credit, 138, 142, 194 sq.
Crime, 118.

DEDUCTION, 183.
Democracy, 138, 141, 142, 171, 232.
Descartes, 184.
Determinism, 73.

INDEX.

Dewey, 86 n.
Differentiation, 47, 69, 99, 144, 169.
Discovery of America, 200.
Division of labor, 145.
Dogmatism, 193, 218.
Domain or territory, 121, 135, 142, 239.
Dynamic Idealism, 25, 36, 48, 147.

EARTH, 37, 52.
Eastern Question, 206 sq.
Endowment-theory, 32, 60, 100, 111.
England, 234.
Environment, 29, 33 sq., 54, 74, 85, 89, 113.
Epiphenomenality, 31, 62, 63.
Equity, 142, 197.
Eternal, 27.
Europe, 51, 141, 176.
Events, 24, 26.
Evil, 222 sq.
Evolution, 30 sq., 77, 82, 203, 217.
Exchange, 173, 189, 190.

FACTORY, 190, 193.
Fatalism, 155, 162.
Feudalism, 182.
Fiatism, 193.
Formalism, 125, 235, 244.
France, 234.
Function, Organic, 67.
Future, 33, 35, 40, 128.

GALILEO, 187.
Genius, 85, 227, 240 sq., 247.
Gentile, 122.
Good, 222 sq.
Government, 134, 142.
Gravity, 100, 101.
Great Man, The, 78, 240 sq.
Greek, 122, 125, 127, 133, 141, 155, 165, 202, 227.
Groot, Hugo de, 176.
Group, 97 sq.

Group, human, or society, 103 sq.

HEAT, 38, 50, 72.
Hegel, 16.
Heraclitus, 201.
Heresy, 193.
History, 11 sq., 43, 56, 77, 92, 97, 130, 211, 222, 249.
History of Philosophy, 16.
Hobbes, 116.

IDEALISM, 198, 236.
Imitation, 241.
Imperialism, 162, 171, 175, 181.
Immortality, 76.
Individualism, 103, 116, 188.
Individuality, 40, 59 sq., 65, 82, 89, 132 sq., 142.
Individuation, 68, 78, 120, 143, 240, 241.
Induction, 183.
Industrialism, 139, 142, 171, 182, 189, 193, 238.
Infinitesimal, 186, 189.
Inheritance, 136, 142, 196.
Inorganic, 60, 84.
Internationalism, 171, 175, 176, 181.
Invasion, 198.
Invention, 241.

JEW, 122, 202, 227, 245, 247.
Judea, 199, 206.

KANT, 62, 185 n.
Kepler, 187.
King, 173.

LABOR or laborer, 132, 142, 145, 151, 152, 173, 177, 190.
Latin, 173, 176.
Law, 45, 91, 135, 138, 142, 155, 157.
Law, International, 176, 197.
Lawfulness, 223 sq.

INDEX.

Lawlessness, 223 sq.
Leadership, 169, 230, 232.
Leibnitz, 187, 188.
Leisure, 151 sq., 227.
Leisured class, 145, 151, 212.
Life and consciousness, 65, 82, 241.
Literature, 133, 136, 140, 142.
Localization, 144.

MACHINERY, 142, 173.
Mallock, 240.
Man, The Great, 78, 240 sq.
Materialism, 58, 73.
Mathematics, 153, 185, 189.
Mechanic, 137, 142.
Mechanicalization, 178, 182, 188, 235.
Mediterannean, 51, 206.
Memory, 33, 203.
Metalism, 193.
Michigan, University of, 37, 38, 52.
Militarism, 142, 169, 171, 189, 238.
Milton, 199.
Miracle, 25, 217.
Monarch, 25, 112, 133, 142, 171, 232.
Money, 135.
Motion, 49.

NATIONALISM, 173, 175, 181.
Nativists, 61.
Naturalism, 155.
Naturalization of the supernatural, 142, 197.
Nature, 54 sq., 120.
Newton, 187.

OCCIDENT, 127, 207.
Officials, 151.
Opinion, Public, 114.
Organic function, 67.
Organism, 23, 35, 36, 47, 75, 84, 86 sq, 98 sq., 104, 189.
Orient, 127, 206.

PAINTING, 199.
Papacy, 112, 173.
Parthians, 150.
Past, 15, 33, 35, 40, 128.
Patriarchism, 133, 142.
Patriotism, 154, 245.
Pericles, 155.
Philosopher, 155, 162, 215.
Philosophy, History of, 16.
Pilgrimage, 199.
Politician, 155, 161.
Positivism, 217.
Present, 15, 40, 128.
Production, 173, 190.
Progress, 80 sq., 93, 200, 201 sq., 246.
Property, 133, 135, 138, 191.
Protestantism, 174, 180, 198, 199.
Public Opinion, 114.

RATIONALISTS, 61.
Realism, 150.
Reason, 211 sq.
Recapitulation, 34, 204.
Religion, 133, 136, 142, 155, 163, 211 sq., 248.
Repetition, 202 sq., 241.
Restoration, 126, 137, 142, 168 sq., 201, 204.
Revelation, 136, 142.
Revolution, 124, 154, 155, 162, 216, 234 sq.; 238.
Rome, 127, 139, 141, 150, 155, 172.
Rousseau, 116.

SCHOLASTICISM, 183.
Schopenhauer, 62.
Science, 9, 31, 45, 155, 160 sq., 217, 227.
Sensationalists, 61.
Sequence, 28, 32, 41, 46, 129.
Servants, 157,
Smith, Adam, 188.
Society, 97, 103.
Socrates, 155, 166, 245.

Soldier, 134, 142, 173, 177.
Sophists, 247.
Sovereignty, 138, 142.
Space, 23, 75, 91.
Spartacus, 179.
Spencer, 103, 105, 112.
Spinoza, 42, 187, 195 n.
Spirit or the spiritual, 26, 57, 76, 134, 142.
Spiritualism, 58.
Stages of Social Evolution, 126, 128, 142.
State, 173.
Sun, as a cause, 37, 52.
Supernatural, 142, 165, 197.

TALENT, 227, 247.
Thinkers or thought, 145, 151, 211 sq.
Time, 21 sq., 75, 85, 91, 203.
Transgressor or transgression, 118, 228, 232.
Transportation, 139, 189.
Travel, 48,
Territory or domain, 121, 135, 142, 239.

UNIVERSITY of MICHIGAN, 37, 38, 52.
Unknowable, 107.

WAR, 238.
Will, 136, 246.
Will, Social, 109, 115, 138.

XERXES, 125.

www.ingramcontent.com/pod-product-compliance
Lightning Source LLC
Chambersburg PA
CBHW021408230426
43666CB00006B/677